Sarah

Tommy Raykovich

ISBN 978-1-63961-761-6 (paperback)
ISBN 978-1-63961-762-3 (digital)

Christian Faith Publishing, Inc.
832 Park Avenue
Meadville, PA 16335
www.christianfaithpublishing.com

Printed in the United States of America

Contents

Acknowledgment

I wish to acknowledge my editor, collaborator, teacher, and friend Marce Welch. Without her help and guidance, this novel would not be what it is today.

1

MARLA FELT A strange sensation. She realized she had lost her focus. Looking down at the speedometer, she saw that she was going way too fast. *Better put the speed control on. It's a long way to South Carolina from Chicago*, she thought. But it was hard for her to focus. She was laid off after six years on the job as a flight attendant for United Airlines because of a stupid virus. *No*, she thought. *How can this be? I worked hard to get to where I was, and now it's gone. And they said they didn't know if I'd ever be hired back again.*

She had graduated from college with a business degree that she knew would not get her much of a job except as a secretary because of her skills. But those skills had worked well on an airplane in flight. Tens of thousands of others like her had also been laid off, and she felt sorry for them and herself as well. But she took a little solace in knowing where she was going. At least—at the very least—she had a place to go. A place to try and figure out what to do next with her life. Waterloo, South Carolina, may not sound like much of a place; but it was special for her. It was where her grandmother lived. Where she grew up.

Marla was an only child at fifteen, when her parents were both killed in a car wreck, and her grandmother took her in to raise her. She hated that time, but she loved that woman. After graduating from high school, she left Waterloo to attend college at Bob Jones University in Greenville, which was not far away. She worked and paid her way. What would have become of her back then? There were no other relatives. But she had to think of the now.

No job; no income. This was not a situation or time to be trying to share an apartment in Chicago. When she called her grandmother, she received a warm welcome and an invitation to live in Waterloo for as long as she wanted to. So she was on her way.

As she turned off the main highway and onto the county road, memories came back. That barn looked familiar… That picket fence was maybe not as white as when she was there last. Oh! She remembered that huge oak tree; and that means that her grandma's house would be just around the curve. When she saw the white wooden farmhouse, it was as if she had lived there only minutes ago, and she felt overwhelmed. As she turned in the driveway, memories of this house, of the time she lived here, all came flooding back. She had to catch her breath. *I'm here. I'm back*, she thought.

Enough of that, Marla thought. *It's just a house, and it was a sad time I don't like to remember. I need a place to stay. That's all. Then I'll move on.* She stopped the car.

Marla opened the car door and stepped out of the Mazda MX-5 Miata like she was stepping out of the cover of *Vogue* magazine. She was a beautiful woman, to say the least. But when describing Marla, the least would not do. She was sculpted and exquisitely adorned. Her features were classic. They spoke for themselves. These attributes had helped get her job. But just that and nothing else. She had virtue; she'd been raised by her parents and her grandmother with the right values. Though she could have gotten a job in modeling and photography, she knew what the bosses would have wanted. Those methods were for others, not for Marla.

With a good-paying job and nothing else to spend her income on, she had indulged herself in fashion. Fashion and Marla were a good couple, and it showed well for both of them. Even showing up at Grandma's house was an event to dress for. She wore a Dolce & Gabbana blouse, which was first shown at a Paris fashion show; Yves Saint Laurent dress pants; and Dior J'Adior sling pumps, which were not suitable for walking on a gravel driveway.

Her hair had been coifed by a stylist before she left the city. Her makeup had been carefully applied. Her skin tone and features needed little improvement. She had bling on her wrists, neck, fingers, waist, and ears. This was Marla. All show. Nevertheless, she showed it well. Walking to the house, she thought of her purse and returned to get it. It was a tan leather Jimmy Choo tote. *I might need something in it,* she thought.

She walked toward the house, uneasy in her steps on the gravel driveway. Walking up the wooden steps to the porch and approaching the screen door felt familiar. She knocked, waited, and then walked in.

Marla saw her grandmother sitting on the couch. A feeling came over her that she did not expect. It made her a little uneasy to feel tears welling up in her eyes. She wanted so much to hug her grandmother. Marla walked toward the woman she loved so dearly and saw that her grandmother was struggling to get up. As Marla slowed her approach, her grandmother rose, eagerly waiting to embrace her. And they did embrace.

"Let me look at you, Dear," Emma said with tears welling up in her eyes. "Marla, you are even more beautiful than I remembered."

Emma hugged her tightly again. "I'm so happy that you've come to stay with me! I can't tell you."

Marla hugged her grandmother. "Grandma, I'm so glad to be here too. Sharing an apartment in Chicago with no job wouldn't have worked. I really didn't want to bother you. I just need time to think and decide on my future. The airlines won't be hiring flight attendants for at least the next two years. I won't be a bother to you. Thanks so much for letting me stay here."

"A bother? Nonsense! You have a room here for as long as you want."

A voice came from behind Marla. "I like your outfit. It looks nice." Marla turned to see a young woman sitting in a chair on the other side of the small room.

I spent a thousand dollars on this outfit, and it looks "nice," she thought. Marla sized her up quickly. Practical straight hair, no makeup, simple housedress. *Plain,* she thought. Then she noticed it. Beside the chair that the woman was sitting in was a motorized scooter chair.

The woman said, "I'm Sarah." Marla noticed that the woman did not rise but lifted her arm from her lap and extended her hand. Marla had a good heart, and pride did not live there.

She walked quickly over to Sarah, firmly taking her hand, and said, "I'm Marla. It's a pleasure to meet you."

"Sarah lives next door. She's my best friend. We spend a lot of time together," her grandmother said.

Sarah looked at the lovely girl as she spoke.

"Yes, Emma and I have developed a great bond over the years. I guess I just wanted a grandmother. I never had one—one that I remember. You and I are about the same age, I guess. I moved here from Greenwood into the house next door after my parents died. We were in an automobile accident when I was sixteen. That's when I lost the use of my legs. I was their only child. They had a little life insurance, and I sold their house. So I have an investment account that will do, if I don't live too long. The house I'm in had been in our family, and I wanted the small-town life…so here I am. The people in this town and in our church have been like a family to me.

"Emma told me you were a flight attendant. That sounds so glamorous! Flying all over the world…"

Sarah was beaming.

"I'm sure you have many stories you could tell! Do you have a boyfriend? I hope you like tea. Emma and I have tea most every afternoon. Oh, Emma, that reminds me… I won't be here tomorrow afternoon. Betty wants me to help at the food pantry. I need to borrow your chocolate-chip cookie recipe. Is that okay? I want to bake them for the church bake sale Saturday. Do you think I should wear my blue dress? Last time I did, Bobby Jo Jenkins wore hers, and we almost looked alike! Marla, you can come to the bake sale, okay? I'll do your hair Friday instead of Saturday, Emma. I want to—"

Emma cut her off. "Sarah, my sakes alive! You can carry on so. Marla just got here and will be here for a while. Save a little for later."

Emma turned to Marla and said, "That girl never met a stranger. I swear she could talk a fence post out of the ground. When she gets started, you better just hang onto your chair."

Sarah, grinning from ear to ear, looked at Emma. "Okay! Okay! Sorry! But I really should go and let you and Marla get her settled in. And you two talk for a while. You know the last thing I would want to do is dominate the conversation. I have laundry in the washer that needs to be dried. I didn't do my ironing yesterday. I need to prepare what I want to take to Laurens tomorrow. I forgot what to study for the Wednesday-night lesson. You'll have to tell me tomorrow, Emma. I wonder where I put my large roasting pan? I'll make a pot roast for us for dinner tomorrow. I guess I better be getting on back home."

Sarah put her hands on the armrest and twisted her body, and it looked like she corkscrewed herself up onto her feet. To Marla, the girl seemed unsteady, and she was reaching out to the girl when Sarah stopped her.

"It's okay. I do this by myself. I can take care of myself. I'm mobile for a few steps. I just can't walk." Sarah grabbed the armrest of the motorized scooter chair. As she twisted around and sat down, she said, "Bye, you two!" Then she started to wheel herself across the room.

It hit Marla. "How—how are you getting out? The steps!"

Sarah replied, "Oh, when Emma and I met, we talked to the men in church. They all pitched in. Jim Fielder, Jimmy Simmons and his two sons, and Pastor Baker, built a ramp out Emma's back door. I had already had ramps put in for my front and back door. Later, after we found it was hard to get across the backyard after it rained, the guys at the lumberyard made the form for a sidewalk, connecting the two ramps in the back. And they paid for the concrete. They are all so nice." She smiled, and there was a thoughtful look in her eyes.

"Well, I'll see you tomorrow!" Then she wheeled herself into the kitchen and out the back door.

"She's something else, isn't she?" Emma said while grinning at Marla, who hesitated, momentarily at a loss for words.

"She seems so happy, carefree for someone in her condition," Marla observed.

Emma replied gently, "She doesn't think of her condition, as you put it. To her, it's just life. She lives life to the fullest. She lets nothing stop her joy." Then both women watched their friend roll down the walkway toward her home.

"Come, Dear, let's get your things and get you settled in your room. Jane Booker brought some of her chicken noodle soup for us for dinner when I told her you were coming today. We'll have it later."

Marla thought to herself, *Sarah lost her parents just like I did at about the same age. But look how differently we turned out. We have something in common.* And there was something about Sarah that intrigued her. Marla had pursued happiness all her life; yet her life was, for the most part, not happy. But this girl, her age and with a similar tragedy in her background, was in a state that Marla did not understand. She was determined to find out more.

2

S HE ROLLED OVER in bed and looked at the clock. The time
was 8:00 a.m. *Gosh*, she thought, *I slept, what, ten hours? I guess
I was more tired than I thought.* She and Emma had talked for
quite a while last night before Emma went to bed at eight. Emma
said she usually went to bed around that time. Marla had stayed up
and looked at her computer for an hour; then, she showered and
turned in.

This was something new for her. With the always changing
flight schedules she worked, sometimes she didn't know if it was
morning or evening. To be able to go to bed in the evening, wake
up in the morning, and not have to go to work or study, was a nice
change from her busy schedule the past ten years. She actually felt
refreshed and relaxed.

Guess I should go and see what Emma is up to.

She went into the bathroom, washed her face, and prepared to
put on her makeup. Then she realized that she didn't have to do this.
But for the beautiful woman she was, having always put on makeup,
she had to apply a little. It didn't seem right not to. She applied a
light moisturizer and just a touch of light foundation. A little light
powder, and then she would do her eyes.

Marla had naturally beautiful eyes; and upon looking in the
mirror, she decided that she would not do anything around her eyes
today. Most women would kill for Marla's long, thick eyelashes and
beautiful brows. After swiping on a light shade of lip color, she was
done. Then she put on her silk La Perla robe and went into the living
room. Emma was sitting on the couch with her knitting.

"Have you been up long?" Marla asked her grandmother.

"Oh, of course, Dear," Emma replied. "I get up every morning at six. Sarah comes over, and we read the Bible together for an hour. She stayed a little longer this morning asking about you. I think she really likes you already. There's coffee in the kitchen. Help yourself. I don't eat breakfast, so if you want something, fix whatever you would like. There are eggs and bacon in the refrigerator."

"I'll just have coffee for now. Thank you," Marla responded.

This is a lot different than what I expected, Marla thought. *I'm going to have to get with the program, I guess.* Actually, she was starting to look forward to a new routine, however different it was from her prior life.

"So what are the plans today?" Marla asked.

"Nothing, Dear," her grandmother replied. "I left today open. I thought we would just talk and catch up on each other. We can go to the market later and get things that you like to eat. My tastes and desires in food are pretty minimal."

"Fine," said Marla. "I need to get into the routine here in Waterloo. I know it will be slower than what I'm used to."

They sat and talked for a long time. Marla talked about working as a flight attendant. It was the same every day: Get on a plane, fly, spend the layover somewhere, sleep, get up the next day, and do it all over again. She did enjoy all the places she got to see during a long layover, and she talked to Emma a lot about all those places. Emma was fascinated.

Her grandmother's life, on the other hand, was much like what Marla thought it would be. Except for the amount of Bible reading and church life that Emma had. With college and her career, Marla had not attended church as an adult. She had grown up with her parents taking her to church every Sunday. They were not involved in their church other than regular Sunday attendance. Marla had been exposed to the Bible and the lessons, and she knew the story. She had just never really given it any thought outside of church. But the seed had been planted. Marla just did not know it yet.

The two women spent a very enjoyable day together. Marla thought a few times how comfortable she felt and how glad and relieved she was that she had come home. It was the right decision, and she felt like a weight had been lifted off her. There was no sense of urgency in looking for another job now.

Sarah came over at about six that evening after dinner. They all settled in the living room with Sarah in her chair, Emma on her side of the couch closest to Sarah, and Marla on the other end of the couch. Emma picked up her knitting and continued working on her project. "What do you do with your time?" Marla asked Sarah.

"Well, I like to stick to a routine. Makes it easier to know where I am. Monday morning, I do my laundry, washing, drying, ironing. Then I do a little light housecleaning. Mrs. Rodriguez comes over that afternoon while I'm gone and does what I can't do. I just don't feel right leaving it all to her. She's such a sweetheart. She won't charge me, but I always leave her what money I can that week. And she's satisfied with it.

"She and her husband have a hard life, working odd jobs to support themselves and their five children. The church helps out sometimes when they can't pay their electric bill. Their kids are so cute! Especially Pedro. I just adore him. Sometimes they'll drop the kids off over here, and we'll watch them when they both need to work and one of them can't be home. Poor things! I wish I could do more for them. She has to wear the same dress to church each Sunday.

"That afternoon, I ride with Sue Jones to one of the assisted-living homes in Laurens, just up the road. We visit with as many of the people living there as we can. Most of them are so lonely and don't have enough visitors. We just talk and read the Bible to them. It makes them so happy! I think if we didn't show up on Monday, Mrs. Reynolds would not last through the night. She's such a dear. Can't hear a word we say, but she enjoys us talking to her anyway. That evening, when we get back, Sue comes in and sits with me, and we talk about our visit that day. It just warms our hearts. Emma, did I tell you her daughter is expecting again?"

Not even looking up from her knitting, Emma said, "Yes, Dear, you did."

"Okay," Sarah said. "Then on Tuesday, Emma and I play Rummy. I let her win most of the time."

Emma chuckled. "You do not! I'm just a better player than you."

Sarah continued, "I paint in the afternoon. I like acrylics, but I have tried some oils."

Emma looked up at Marla. "Marla, you need to see her paintings. She's quite good."

"Oh, Emma, I am not! I just enjoy it."

"Then why does everyone in town have one of your paintings in their home?" Emma asked.

"Well, I do like painting," Sarah said. "Where was I? Emma, you talk so. I don't know where I was. Tuesday, I think. Well, on Wednesday, Mary Scott picks me up, and we go to the library in Laurens and help them. They love volunteers. The library has a staff, but they can only do so much. The city pays the bills but can't afford a regular staff. Everyone does what they can. I love to read. Do you like to read, Marla?"

Marla started to answer, but she was not fast enough.

"We get back around four in the afternoon, and we each get ready for Wednesday night Bible study and fellowship and dinner at the church. One of the ladies picks me and Emma up. They have some system, I guess. We never know who, but someone always does. You'll have to come with us, Marla!

"Emma, did they ever fix the stove? It is hard to get everything prepared with only two burners working. I liked listening to Bill Johnson give the lesson last week. He's such a good speaker. I don't know who buys his clothes, though. He always picks the wrong shirt for the pants he's wearing since his wife passed away. Thursday, Millie Smith takes me and Emma to the market to get groceries. The three of us have such a good time. That Millie sure is a talker!"

Emma, not looking up from her knitting, just shook her head from side to side and smiled.

"We can spend a half an hour discussing which apple is the best to take home. By the time we have each gotten what we need, and she brings us home, it's lunchtime. She's such a dear. She always unloads the groceries, brings them in for each of us, and helps us put them away. I just love her new hairstyle! Don't you, Emma?"

"Yes, Dear," Emma replied.

"I wish she hadn't colored it. I liked it the color it was," Sarah went on. "In the afternoon is when I work on my embroidery. Emma, you need to come see the new patterns I got off the internet. I can't wait to get on them. I have to finish my pillowcase I'm doing for Pastor Baker. His birthday's coming up. You haven't forgotten have you, Emma?"

"No, Dear. I remember," Emma said.

"Remember, we said we would bake the cake for his surprise party. Where was I? Oh! Friday, Bill Perkins comes over and does my yardwork, and I sit on the front porch and talk to him while he's working. I guess I have more that needs to be done than other people whose yards he tends to. He's always saying how long it takes him at my house."

Emma shook her head from side to side again.

"That afternoon, I have a list of people who live alone in the county, and I call them up and talk and cheer them up. They all seem to like it. They stay on the line a long time."

At this, Marla looked over at Emma, but she didn't shake her head this time. She just looked at Marla and winked.

"Saturday, I leave open, and Emma and I just sit and talk."

"I mostly listen," Emma said.

"Oh, that's not true, Emma," Sarah said. "You talk when I'm not talking. Then it's Sunday, and that day belongs to our Lord. I spend it with him. Reading, worshipping, and thanking him, in church and at home."

Marla suddenly realized that Sarah was not going to say anything. *I better get a word in edgewise while I can*, Marla thought. "My goodness, Sarah! How do you do all that? I'm worn out just thinking about all you do." Marla was going to continue, but she hesitated for a second too long.

Sarah had started again. "Oh, I just like to stay busy. God has blessed me, and I just want to give back to him."

Sarah continued talking.

Marla was deep in thought. She knew she didn't have to help carry the conversation. Her gaze was fixed on the other, whose mouth was moving. Marla was getting most of the conversation, but her mind was on something else. Her mind was on Sarah, the woman, not the conversation.

Marla thought that Sarah was the most remarkable woman she had met, and she had met many. But looking back, she saw how shallow most of them were. They were one person on the surface and someone else inside. But not Sarah. With her, what you saw was what you got. Sarah was real; there was nothing phony about this girl.

For a moment, Marla felt a little jealous. How had Sarah discovered the thing that Marla had searched for but not yet found? There was a happiness which had eluded Marla. No, it was more than that. It was something else, but Marla didn't know what. She realized that she was starting to like Sarah and wanted to know more about her.

3

SHE GOT UP and dressed earlier the next morning so that she could be with Sarah and her grandmother while they were reading the Bible.

"I'm so glad you joined us this morning," Emma said. "Come, sit beside me. We're reading in the book of James."

Marla sat down beside her grandmother.

"Go on, Sarah," Emma said.

"'What good is it, my brothers and sisters, if someone claims to have faith but has no deeds? Can such faith save them? Suppose a brother or a sister is without clothes and daily food. If one of you says to them, "Go in peace; keep warm and well fed," but does nothing about their physical needs, what good is it? In the same way, faith by itself, and not accompanied by action, is dead. But someone will say, "You have faith; I have deeds." Show me your faith without deeds, and I'll show you my faith by my deeds.

'You believe that there is one God. Good! Even the demons believe that—and shudder. You foolish person, do you want evidence that faith without deeds is useless? Was not our father Abraham considered righteous for what he did when he offered his son Isaac on the altar? You see that his faith and his actions were working together, and his faith was made complete by what he did. And the scripture was fulfilled that says, "Abraham believed God, and it was credited to him as righteousness; and he was called God's friend. You see that a person is considered righteous by what they do and not by faith alone."'"

Marla interrupted. "Excuse me. Can I ask a question?"

Sarah stopped reading.

"Of course, Dear," Emma stated.

"I remember being taught that we are saved by faith, and that is it," Marla stated. "We don't have to do anything else. I believe in God." Marla stopped.

Sarah responded, "Yes, Marla, that's correct. But our faith has to be greater than that. God is love. He loves us, and he wants us to love him, not just believe that he exists. When you love someone, you want the best for them. You want to give to them and do for them. God feels that way for us. And when we love him, that's what he does. He gives to us.

"God isn't something we believe in. He's a companion in our lives, a companion we love. Because we love him, we want to give back to him what he gives to us. Not because he needs it or expects it but because we love him. That's why we, Emma and me and most other Christians, work for God every day. It's because we love him."

Sarah stopped talking. Marla's mind stopped working. It was as if time had stopped. No one had ever talked to her like that or about this subject. She didn't know what to think, what to say, or what to believe. She felt like she was in the presence of someone much, much better than she was. This "plain" woman had spoken to her heart, and she didn't know how to respond.

"Marla," the girl said in a softer voice and tone, "I know you're a believer. I'm glad for that. Your grandmother told me of your past and your exposure to the Word in church and in your youth. There's so much more...*so* much more. Oh, Marla, the wonders of God are immense, and he wants the best for you! You just have to turn your life over to him and trust him. He knows what's best for you."

Marla was stunned. She felt so small in the presence of Sarah. Plain Sarah. Marla felt tears welling in her eyes. "Sarah, I...I...thought...I...thought...I don't know what I thought. Oh, Sarah, I have so much to learn!"

Marla didn't know if she should voice her next request, but it came out anyway.

"Will you teach me?"

She stopped. She couldn't believe she had said that. A woman of the world who thought she was on top of it a month ago was, in that moment, asking for help from this woman, Sarah. Plain Sarah.

In the small town of Waterloo, South Carolina. *What has happened to my world*, Marla wondered?

"Yes," Sarah replied.

One word and no more. Marla was glad that she had said yes. She looked over at her grandmother, who had a knowing smile. Marla then realized that hers and Sarah's relationship had taken a new turn.

S ARAH HAD ASKED her new friend to come with her to the county food pantry and help. "Go put on some old clothes. Billie Jean will be here in a few minutes."

By then, they had already finished their Bible reading for the morning.

"Okay," Marla said as she left the room. She went into her room to look for something to put on. *Christian Dior shorts. They are old,* she thought. *But what blouse would go with them?* She didn't know how to dress for Waterloo, South Carolina.

As she went back into the living room, Sarah looked at her, surprised, and broke into a chuckle.

"What are you laughing at?" Marla asked, slightly perturbed.

"You. I'm laughing at you!" Sarah said. "Those are *old* clothes?"

"Well, I haven't worn them in over a year," Marla stated emphatically.

"Fine. After today, you will probably never wear them again. Come on. Let's go. Billie Jean is waiting." Sarah snickered again.

Marla wondered, *I haven't seen her laugh like that. Is she really laughing at me?* It was a day to remember for all concerned.

It was good that Marla had a sense of humor. She wondered all day, *Why is everyone in such a good mood today? They are all laughing most of the time.* But really, she did enjoy that day. Seeing all the people in need come in to get the assistance and all the people willing to help them struck a chord in her heart.

But what she admired and enjoyed the most was watching Sarah when she had a chance. Sarah was in her wheelchair, doing her best to help pass out boxes of food. Sarah had a wheelchair for when she was away from her house. Whoever she was with would push her where she wanted to go.

The whole time they were there, Marla could not remember a moment when Sarah was not deep in conversation with the people in need. But she was not just rambling on, as she was known to do. She was engaging all she met, asking how they were doing. She knew them all by name, and she knew all their problems and expressed a heartfelt compassion to each and every one.

Marla had never witnessed such love for others as Sarah showed. Something stirred inside Marla as she thought of it. She felt a twinge of compassion. It felt good. At the end of the day, she felt for the first time in her life that she had really accomplished something worthwhile, and it showed on her clothes.

"Well," she told Sarah when they got home, "I guess I have some old clothes now!"

"Marla," Sarah said as they all finally got into Emma's living room, "I think tomorrow, you and I should go to Walmart in Laurens and buy you a new wardrobe."

This time, it was Marla who chuckled.

"What are you laughing at?" Sarah asked, slightly puzzled.

"Sarah, I have always bought my clothes in the finest boutiques in large cities in the States and overseas. And now I am to buy 'a new wardrobe' at, of all places, Walmart!" Marla chuckled again.

"Yes, well, you see, Marla, those clothes you bought were for the old Marla in those cities. You're in our world now here in Waterloo. I don't think anyone here would even know what fashion is. Here, everything is *practical*, especially our clothes," Sarah said, emphasizing practical.

"I guess you're right," Marla admitted. She knew that when it came to practical, Sarah was her better. *Another lesson from plain Sarah*, Marla thought.

"Okay, tomorrow we go to Walmart! I've heard about that place. Just don't take any pictures of me in there," Marla joked.

The next day, the girls piled into the Miata and headed to Laurens, the closest town that had a Walmart. They left Sarah's wheelchair since it wouldn't fit in the car, and Walmart had motorized shopping carts for their customers. They talked and talked all the way there. Marla felt like she had known Sarah all her life. She was so comfortable and at ease when she was with her friend now.

Once at the Walmart parking lot, Marla went in and got a cart for Sarah, and they went back inside. They had such a time up and down the aisles at Walmart. Sarah told Marla what she was to buy, and Marla did not question anything. She was confident that Sarah was in her world and knew more about this than she did.

They got a few pairs of jeans, shorts, blouses, and T-shirts for everyday wear. A few nicer things for special occasions in Waterloo. A bathrobe and a couple pairs of pajamas rounded out the wardrobe. The girls also picked out two simple purses, one for every day and a nicer one for special occasions in Waterloo. After picking out a few undergarments, off they went to the shoe department. They took a couple pairs of simple walking shoes and a couple pairs of flats for special occasions.

"No heels," Sarah explained. "You walk mostly on God's earth in Waterloo. Not so much concrete here." Marla also wanted to check out the jewelry, but Sarah would have none of it. "Waste of money," she simply told Marla. Then they got in line to check out.

The cashier told Marla that the total was $348.43. Marla looked at her and asked if she missed something. "No," the cashier replied.

Marla put her credit card in the machine, and while it was processing, she turned to Sarah. "I used to spend that much on a single blouse, and now I can buy a *new wardrobe* for that!"

Sarah laughed out loud. "That blouse was not practical, Marla!" she said, still laughing.

After wardrobe shopping, they went over to the lunch counter to grab a bite to eat. They were both in good spirits, and the conversation was lively. Marla was learning how to talk to Sarah. It was like getting into a swimming pool—you just dive right in. As they were getting into the car, after cramming her purchases into the Miata, Marla thought that she could not remember when she had, had more fun with someone. She had such a good feeling inside. It almost made her giddy.

"Sarah, I've been thinking," Marla started. "My car isn't practical here. I bought it on a whim, paid cash for it, and it's only six months old. I'm going to sell it and buy a good used SUV so I can take you and your chair and my grandmother wherever you want to go. I think I'd come out ahead on the trade if I could find the right used car, and I'd like the extra cash right now. It's the practical thing to do."

Sarah felt a lump in her throat. People were always doing things for her and being nice to her, but this was different. Marla was not selling a car for her; rather, she was giving up a way of life for her. For Sarah and Emma. *Marla is starting to reveal her heart to me*, Sarah thought. She felt a bond developing between them.

"Marla, that's the nicest thing anyone's ever done for me! I know this is more than just a car to you. It would be such a blessing to me and Emma, not having to always ask someone to take us everywhere, even though we know they don't mind. Are you sure about this?" Sarah asked.

"Positive," Marla answered. "I want to go to the car dealer while we're here and see what they have in used cars. Do you mind waiting in the car? I'll tell the salesperson that we can't stay long today. What do you say?"

"I'm with you, Marla. Lead the way," Sarah answered.

Marla drove to the car lot, got out, and went in to get a salesperson. Sarah watched them as they went over to the used cars and talked a little. Then they came over to where Sarah and the Miata were, and he looked it over.

They went inside, and Marla came back a few minutes later.

"Well, I think we're in business! He has a small six-year-old SUV with only seventy thousand miles on it. It will suit the three of us just fine. He'll give me a good price for my car, and I'll have a nice sum left over after the exchange. He's going to go over the final figures and call me later today. If everything is okay, I'll make the trade in the next day or two. What do you think, Miss Practical?" Marla asked, grinning.

"I think I'm dreaming," Sarah said, grinning back at her. "You're the practical one now. Thank you, Marla."

They drove out of the dealership and headed home. Both remained quiet, each reflecting on the events of what had been a great day.

Sarah looked at her friend and spoke firmly and slowly, "I love you, Marla."

Marla felt a tear in her eye. No one except her mother and father had ever said those words to her. Marla responded, "I love you too, Sarah."

They were each thoughtful on the way home. Neither had, had a sister or even a best friend when growing up. They each truly enjoyed being in the company of the other, and each was looking forward to this new relationship. They could not wait to tell Emma.

S THE DAYS rolled on, the two women were inseparable. Everywhere Sarah went, Marla was beside her. Each time they were together, it was like the best of friends had been apart for a year and were back together again. They were a pair, to be sure. Everyone in town noticed it, and all were so happy for both of them. They knew Sarah and what a heart she had—always giving but always alone, never with someone her age. Fortunately, Marla had fit right in with the community.

Marla knew how to interact with and engage others. She had had six years of on-the-job training. As a flight attendant, this was part and parcel of her trade. Marla knew how to make friends, and friends she did make in Waterloo. She remembered well that first Sunday after the Walmart wardrobe trip, when she went to church with Sarah and her grandmother. No one knew her at the time; but when she was introduced to anyone by Sarah or Emma, she was treated like she was part of their family. A loving and caring family. She had never felt so welcome in her life. After that, she never felt like a stranger again. She was always meeting or being introduced to someone new, and soon she was part of Waterloo.

But there was a change stirring within Marla. She was not really aware of it any more than you are aware of new shoes after you have gotten used to them. Something was happening deep inside, in a place where Marla had not spent much time before coming to Waterloo. She had always been focused on the exterior; it showed upon her arrival. But she began to change the moment Sarah came into her life. The beauty that was Marla, the fashion that she indulged in, the glamor of her job, all were part of a façade. Nowadays, though, she was spending her time on other things; and the façade was slowly disappearing.

Sarah had convinced her a week after the Walmart trip that she should change her hairstyle. It was long, and Marla had to spend much time on it every day. It was a fashion thing and was not practical. Reluctantly agreeing, she got a chic short haircut, which was still stylish but low in maintenance. Marla liked it immediately. Change was something that she didn't have a problem with if it was for the better. Each morning, when she got ready for the day and looked at herself in the mirror, she realized that she liked the new Marla more.

And then there was the makeup. Sarah put her foot down on this one, and they had a few friendly discussions before Marla gave in. Once again, though, she knew that Sarah was right. It wasn't practical, and it was expensive. Sarah just pointed out Marla's natural beauty and eventually convinced her to let it show.

As the weeks went by, Marla saw her old self, the one from Chicago, slowly fading. Soon, it would become only a memory. But she really did not give it much thought since she and Sarah were so busy with life in Waterloo each day. The Marla persona from Chicago was dying. A new Marla had been conceived and would be born soon, when God was ready. Marla was living each day as the best day.

Marla had been to church every Sunday morning and every Wednesday evening. She was with Sarah and her grandmother each morning for Bible reading. When Sarah went to Bible study, Marla was with her. And Marla was like a sponge soaking it all in. But you cannot read and comprehend the Bible within a few weeks. You cannot attend a few sermons and get the totality of the message of the Word.

Marla had the best teacher anyone could have had in Sarah. She recalled herself saying after the first Bible reading, "Will you teach me?" At that point, she already knew that Sarah had meant it when she had said yes. When Sarah said she would do something, there was no questioning whether or not it would happen. And to Sarah, this was much more special. This was about the heart and soul of someone she loved like her own sister.

Sarah devoted her all to bringing Marla closer to God, and it showed. Marla knew she was learning daily about praying and worshipping and serving the Lord.

"**L**ET'S GO ON a picnic after church," Sarah said one day. "The state park on Lake Greenwood is only twenty-five minutes away, and it's such a beautiful day."

"That sounds wonderful! I can't remember when I went on a picnic," Marla replied. She thought, *We have been so busy lately. It would be nice to just relax for an afternoon.*

"We'll just take whatever we have in the refrigerator. I'll make some tea to take. Does that sound okay?" Sarah asked.

"Fine with me," Marla replied.

As soon as they arrived home from church, Marla started packing the food, blankets, and picnic supplies. Emma wasn't feeling well, and she really didn't want to interfere anyway. She knew this would be good for the two of the them, to just spend time together. They were always together, but they were always doing something for others. Marla packed the SUV with everything she thought they might need or want. Afterward, they piled themselves into the SUV and were gone. This put both of them in good spirits, and the talk on the way to the state park was lively.

They got a handicap site at the office and finally headed for their spot. Sarah was right. It was a beautiful day, and they got themselves the perfect spot for a picnic. They could look out over the lake. Marla set everything up, including two sturdy chairs that she had brought. She then fixed her friend a plate of food, took it to her, and fixed one for herself. They sat looking at the lake, enjoying their meal.

They ate quietly for a few minutes, enjoying the scenery and the moment. Then Sarah spoke first.

"I'm so glad you came to live with us here. It's nice to have someone my age to talk to! I love everyone in Waterloo, and Emma is really like a grandmother to me. But I feel my life is complete with you as my friend. I know I can ramble on when talking; but I just wanted to tell you how much better my life is now that you're here."

Once again, Sarah had taken the air out of Marla. After a moment, Marla had composed herself.

Trying not to cry, she said softly, "Oh, Sarah, you don't know the half of it! In Chicago and at work… I never had any friends. Acquaintances, colleagues, companions—nothing more. No one I could trust, no one I really wanted to be with. Losing my job was the second-best thing that ever happened to me. It brought me to Waterloo. But meeting you was the best thing that ever happened to me."

Marla got up and put her plate down on her chair. Then she stepped over to give Sarah, her friend, a hug. Sarah reached out with one arm and put her hand on Marla's arm. They both started to cry.

"Okay, that's enough. You're making me cry, and it's getting my potato chips wet and soggy! Let's just sit here and enjoy the peace and quiet. We're in God's country now," Sarah said. "This is the best afternoon I've ever spent. Thank you for bringing us here."

That's a joint opinion, Marla thought to herself as Sarah spoke it.

They rode home together engaging in casual conversation. Sarah didn't speak much. They both felt peace in their hearts. Someone had been watching over them, and it felt good having a best friend and a sister.

Sarah had planned a special time to help Sue Jones with a surprise party for Mrs. Reynolds, one of their friends at the assisted-living home. Sarah was giving it, and others were helping; so Marla was alone on the back porch with a cup of coffee, thinking. She didn't have many moments alone to think like this. Her mind was clear, and she didn't have to engage in conversation with Sarah, which was sometimes like being a kite in the wind or being carried along by the current of a river on a raft with no rudder or paddle. She loved Sarah dearly, but this was a nice morning alone; and she was going to enjoy it with her own thoughts.

She reflected on the last three months… *What a transition!* It took her breath away to think of the woman who drove from Chicago compared to the woman she was now. She had no regrets about losing her Chicago life. That woman of her past wasn't real. For the first time in her life, Marla felt real. It was partly because of the "practical changes" that Sarah had suggested. But mostly it was because of the real changes that Sarah had caused to happen in her life. And she loved Sarah even more for those changes.

She still could not comprehend how someone like Sarah could have caused such a profound change in her life. *What is it about this simple, plain woman that is making such an impact on me?* Marla wondered. *What makes Sarah different?* She knew instantly. It was her heart. Not the one pumping blood through her body, but the inner heart.

Why does Sarah have such a compassionate heart? Marla wondered. Part of it had to do with beauty. Marla knew about beauty—outer beauty. No one did it better than Marla back then. But Sarah's *inner* beauty was far better. It was beautiful to God because it was of God. Marla had focused on having beauty for the benefit of those people who saw her. People who didn't understand or care about her inner beauty. People who didn't even know that such a thing as inner beauty existed.

What a waste of time those years were, Marla thought. *What do I have to show for them?* A profound feeling of sadness came over her. She'd spent so much money and so many hours focusing on the exterior aspects of her life. The pursuit of happiness.

"My God, yes! That's what I did all those years! Pursue my own happiness. And I never found it."

Marla, for the first time in her life, realized what she had lost. She could earn money again. But she could never get back the time.

"What a waste!" she said out loud. "That was not practical. In fact, it was stupid, simple and…plain."

Marla realized she was poor. She had little to show for the resources she had invested and spent. But look at Sarah's estate. She was far richer than Marla! Marla had worked for herself and her own benefit. Sarah was working for God and his kingdom. It was suddenly obvious to Marla that her friend's reward was much better than any she had ever thought. A light glowed brighter within Marla. She didn't see it, but it was glowing in her heart. It was real, and it had begun to direct her life—the life that God had planned when he'd first planted the seed of faith in her all those years ago.

7

T WAS A typical Sunday morning in their church for the 11:00
a.m. worship service. Emma was sitting in her regular pew in the
last row on the outside. That was so that Sarah could sit beside
her, and Sarah's wheelchair could be put off to the side and not block
an aisle.

Sarah, as usual, was wheeling herself all over the sanctuary and
carrying on conversations with anyone she could corner. She knew
how to corner people with that wheelchair, but no one minded. That
was Sarah, and they all loved her for it. If you didn't get cornered by
Sarah and get to visit with her, well, you just missed out on it that
Sunday. Marla was making the rounds as they all did, engaging in
friendly conversation before the service began.

Ed Fielding approached her as she was talking to Mary Gibbons,
the church secretary. They were just chit-chatting. But Marla was
aware that Ed was standing beside them, waiting. Ed was a good man,
quite handsome, a few years older than Marla, but never married. He
was a pillar of the church—an elder, on the board of deacons, and on
the church advisory committee. He taught Sunday school if it were
asked of him. He approached Marla.

"Can I have a word with you after church? I'd just like to discuss
something with you," he said.

"Of course, Ed."

Marla left it at that. After the service was over, Marla told Emma
and Sarah that Ed wanted to talk to her and that she would be with
them when she could.

"Of course," they both said. Off Sarah went to corner someone.

Ed and Marla found each other after the usual conversations
with others after the service. "Let's go to the library," Ed said. He led

the way, and Marla followed. When they were both in the library, Ed started.

"You know I have my own insurance business. Well, my business has grown over the last two years beyond what I can manage by myself. I have to be on the road going to see clients, daily filling out paperwork at night at home, constantly on the phone. I can't do all this and grow my business. But I love what I do, and I know there's a lot of insurance business I can get in this county. So I've decided to open an office and formally start my own insurance agency. I need someone to run that office.

"I've come to know you over the last few months and know that you have the talents, abilities, and knowledge to handle what I need. Marla, I'd like to hire you to work for me and run my office. I know that you and Sarah are so involved in our church and community, and I would allow you the time to continue your work in those capacities. We would start out with flexible hours so you could do what you want to do. I'm just getting started, and the office would only need to be open a few days a week for a few hours to start. We could build from there. I'll pay you a good salary. What do you think?"

Marla thought to herself, *I can't think now. That's what I think.* In the next few seconds, her life for the last six months flashed before her eyes. Flying all over the world, being laid off, driving to Waterloo, getting away for a while, and resolving to get a job later. Then meeting Sarah, making a friend, being involved in a church and God's work.

Reality. New life. Flashback over.

"Ed, yes! Yes! The work sounds interesting, and I want to help my grandmother. Oh, Ed, are you sure you want me? I don't know anything about the insurance business."

"I know that," Ed said, "but I've learned to recognize your qualities and capabilities, in both the personal and business sense. I know you are a smart lady and a good woman. I'll teach you all you need to know. Bill Reynolds has an old building in town he's been sitting on for a long time and would love to rent. He said he would pay for the remodel since it needs some work if I sign a long-term lease, which

I'd be glad to do. I love this town, this community, this county, and I want to build my business here. We could do it together. How does that sound?"

Marla thought, *I've never had a better offer in my life.* "It sounds good," she answered.

"I'll call you at the end of the week. Bill said he could have a contractor start on the building soon. Let's exchange mobile numbers and information, and I'll call you."

Marla went back and found Sarah and Emma waiting for her. Most people had already left the church.

"Well, what was that about?" Sarah asked as soon as Marla got close.

"Oh, not much. Ed is thinking of opening an office for his insurance business and may want to hire me to run the office for him," Marla said, acting nonchalant about it but barely able to control her enthusiasm.

Emma smiled. Sarah was practically speechless, but she did manage to say, "Oh, Marla, that's great! I'm so happy for you. I know you want to work. Ed is a fine man. I don't think you could find a better boss—or probably a better job—in Laurens County."

"Every week in Waterloo, it seems, something good happens!" Marla stated, her enthusiasm showing now.

"It's just part of God's plan for you, Marla. I told you if you would trust God, he knows what's best for you. He wants the best for you," Sarah stated calmly.

Marla thought, *That must be right. Sarah said it.*

The three of them left and drove home. On the way home, the three women were all talking at the same time, all full of joy.

E D CALLED THAT next Friday.

"Marla, it's all working out better than I had hoped. Bill must really need the rent money. He got the contractor to finish the work ahead of schedule, and it's ready for us. We have new carpet, new paint, remodeled bathroom. He even had internet and phone connections put in. Can you meet me there Monday morning? It's across the highway from the hardware store. Say, nine o'clock?"

"Absolutely!" Marla said, barely able to control her excitement. "I can't wait! Thank you so much, Ed. You don't know how much this means to me. I'll be the best office manager you ever had."

"You'll be the only office manager I ever had," Ed said jokingly. "But I've no doubt about the 'best' part. We'll make a great team, Marla."

Marla had a thought for a split second but let it go. "I'll see you Monday. And thanks again, Ed. Goodbye."

"Goodbye, Marla."

*****

Monday morning could not come soon enough for Marla. While getting ready for her first day on the job, she thought that she was glad Sarah was not here. Marla had pulled out some of her clothes from Chicago that had been put away after she had purchased the new wardrobe at Walmart. She didn't want anything too fancy but just a professional business look. *Something practical*, she thought.

Then she went into the bathroom to apply some makeup; but this morning, it would be just a tad more than subtle. This time she went with the eye treatment that she seldom applied anymore:

mascara, not too heavy; subtle application of eyeliner; just a little color to the eyebrows. The finished look was minimal but stylish. "I don't think Sarah would mind, under the circumstances," she said to herself.

She put on her blouse and pants then went back to the bathroom to put on a little lip color. Finishing off with a pair of the nice flats Sarah had picked out for her would be perfect. After putting the contents of her everyday purse into her nicer purse, she was off.

It was hard to be late to anything in Waterloo, which was only a dot on the map. She arrived at ten 'til nine, and Ed was already there. He was carrying some boxes from his car.

Upon getting out of her car, she said, "Can I help you?"

"No," he replied, "this is the last of it. Come on in."

Marla walked in behind him and could not believe her eyes. It was beautiful. They could still smell the fresh paint. There was a simple front room with a hall leading to the back of the building from the left side of the room. In this room was a desk, a chair, a filing cabinet, bookshelves, and a couch for clients. There was a side table by the couch with a lamp on it.

"Ed, how did you do all this? You have everything but magazines on the table."

"Decorating is a woman's job. The magazines are your responsibility," Ed said, smiling. "When Bill told me early Friday that the building would be ready, I borrowed the delivery van from Fred at the hardware store, drove to Greenwood, and bought the furniture. Fred and his two employees helped me set it all up Saturday afternoon. I have my office in the first room to the right down the hall with the basics for a small office.

"Marla, I've been dreaming and planning on this for quite some time now. I had the money saved for when I knew I would need to do this. The only thing missing was someone I knew who was capable, who I could trust to work with me. I knew after I had met you, and had been around you a few times, that you were the one I'd been waiting for. To be honest, it just took me until last Sunday to get up the nerve to ask you."

You're a special woman, and I'm just an ordinary guy, Ed thought.

38

Marla started blushing. "Ed, that's the sweetest, nicest thing anyone has ever said to me."

She impulsively reached out and gave him a gentle hug; then, she immediately took a step back. "I'm sorry. I shouldn't have done that," Marla said awkwardly.

"That's all right, Marla. I'm glad you did," Ed replied, not wanting to sound too forward. "Come over here, and let me show you your office."

Taking one step forward, he waved his hand in a sweeping motion. The tension was over.

"I bought you a computer, a monitor, a printer, the needed accessories, and a landline phone. I assumed you would know how to hook everything up. The internet router is on top of the bookcase. I'm going to call on a couple of clients, and I'll be back later. When I get back, you can take my credit card and go the Dollar General for whatever basic office supplies you need to get started. I need to set up my desk and office. Maybe then we could grab some lunch and talk for a while?" Ed said wistfully.

In her mind, Marla pinched herself. *I've got to be dreaming*, she thought. At a loss for words, she simply said, "That sounds great."

Ed said goodbye and was out the door. By then, Marla's only thought was *I've got to sit down. I'm shaking all over!* She realized that she had a lunch date with a good, handsome man. This time she really did pinch herself on the arm. Then she got to work hooking up the electronics.

Ed came back a couple of hours later when Marla was just about finished with her setup. He gave her his credit card, and she went to the Dollar General for office supplies. She came back and walked in carrying her purchases. Ed heard her come in and came to the front.

"Do you have more?" he asked.

"Yes," Marla replied.

They walked out to Marla's car together; and between the two of them, they were able to bring in the rest of the bags.

"They didn't have everything I think I'll need. I bought some things for your office too. I hope I didn't spend too much, Ed."

"You couldn't have spent too much at the Dollar General, and I know we have to spend money to get this office functional. You can make a list of what we need for both our offices and the rest of the building, and we can go to Greenwood later this week to get it and be done. Then we can both get to work. Why don't we go to lunch, and you can unpack when we get back?" Ed said, smiling.

Marla smiled back and said, "Okay."

"We'll take my car," Ed said.

They walked out; and as Marla approached the passenger side, Ed stepped in front of her and opened the door.

"Thank you," Marla said. As Ed walked around the front of the car, Marla pinched herself again. *I don't care if that did hurt. I know I'm dreaming*, she thought. *No one has ever treated me like he does.*

9

THE GOLF CLUB close by just had a grill, but it offered good food. Mondays were slow days at the golf course, so they were the only customers. Bart Sessions was working the grill.

"Morning, Ed," they heard as they walked in.

"Morning, Bart," Ed replied.

Bart was not a shy guy. When he saw Marla walk in with Ed, his attention was off of whatever trivial thing he was working on at the time.

"My goodness, Missy, you're about the prettiest thing I think ever came in here! Matter of fact, you're probably the prettiest thing I've ever seen. You're not from around here, are you? I wouldn't have forgotten if I'd seen you before."

Then Bart remembered his wife. "Ed, don't you tell Marsha I said that," Bart said, laughing.

"Bart, I didn't hear a word you said," Ed replied.

Marla blushed a little. This was honest flattery, not the kind of comments she used to get.

"I'm Marla, Emma's granddaughter, and I'm staying with her. I've been here a few months, and I've heard about this golf course but have never been out here."

"Well, I hope you'll come back again," Bart said. "You brighten this place up better than a bouquet of flowers. Y'all sit where you want. I'll fetch you some water and menus. Be right there!"

They went to a table by a window. Ed held her chair for her and slid it forward as she sat down. "Don't worry about Bart. He's harmless," Ed said. "He likes to carry on, but he's been happily married to his wife, Marsha, for over thirty-five years."

Bart brought the menus and water. Ed looked at Marla and asked, "Cheeseburger and fries okay with you? It's the only thing you can be sure Bart won't burn."

"Well, I've heard about your cooking, Ed," Bart countered. "My worst is better than your best any day."

Marla chuckled and said, "That'll be fine."

"Okay, just go start cooking our lunch. We don't have all day," Ed said, smiling back at Bart. Then Bart grabbed the menus and was off.

"I'll confess, Marla. He's right about my cooking. I eat out most of the time or eat something frozen or already prepared."

"Well, from all I know about you, that's the only flaw I've seen or heard of. No one's perfect."

They had a nice, quiet lunch. Marla told Ed about her family and her history with Waterloo. She also talked about college, the airlines, why she was here. He was fascinated with her career and said that he wanted to hear more about it later. Ed told Marla that he had grown up in Greenwood and gone to Lander University there. He could live at home and basically walk to campus unless the weather was bad (his family didn't have the money to pay room and board somewhere else). Once he graduated, he went to work at an insurance agency in Greenwood, where he learned the trade.

He had liked the insurance business and was good at it. The man he worked for told him so, he told Marla. He knew he could run his own business someday, but he needed to be where there was virtually no competition. So he moved to Waterloo since there was no large insurance agency outside the cities in Laurens County. He'd never married because he couldn't find a good woman that met his standards. Besides, with his college studies and then learning the insurance business, he didn't have time for romance. He also said that he'd been a Christian since he was a young boy, when he'd accepted Jesus. God had blessed him.

Marla couldn't take her eyes off him while he spoke. She'd been on many dates in her life, not many of them worth remembering. She knew why now. She had always been around shallow men who always put up the masculine screen to hide all the flaws and imperfections that existed beneath that deceit. But Ed was different. Now, for the first time in her life, she could recognize the difference. Ed was honest, humble, and real. And this wasn't a dream. Her life was really happening, and God was making it better every day. She had to admit to herself that she was going to enjoy working with Ed.

They stayed and talked for an hour, and they each knew why. For the first time in each of their lives, they were comfortable and enjoying the company of someone of the opposite sex. They went back to the office and worked for another hour or two. Afterward, Ed told Marla to come back on Wednesday morning, and he would begin her training. They would transfer all his files to her computer, and she would be able to start helping him with all the paperwork.

It was a start. In fact, it was a start to a *lot* of things.

As each drove home, they both had a similar thought: *Thank you, Lord. It's been a really great day.* They could not wait for Wednesday to get back to the office.

10

MARLA GOT HOME at about 4:30 p.m. and found Sarah and her grandmother sitting in the living room, each in her usual place. Emma was working on her knitting, and Sarah was doing her part by telling Emma many things that she already knew or that Sarah had already told her. Emma loved every word and would have taken a cane switch to anyone who tried to stop Sarah. Marla walked in wearing a happy smile. They both thought how beautiful she was.

Sarah couldn't resist. "Looking kind of prissy today, aren't you?" she said with a grin on her face.

"Sarah, I'm working in an office, and this was my first day. I just wanted to make a good impression," Marla countered.

"Well, if I was Ed, it would've impressed me," Sarah said, grinning even more.

"Sarah, I swear I might come over there and swat you one!" Marla said, grinning in the same way as Sarah was.

"Oh, you two, stop it!" Emma stated, starting to grin with them. "I want to hear about Marla's day."

"I do too, Miss Prissy," Sarah said, looking directly at Marla and laughing out loud.

"I've a good mind to tell Emma and not you, so there!" Marla responded to Sarah.

They bantered back and forth like this every day, each trying to better the other. After a while, Marla gave up. *She got me again*, she thought.

"Oh, come over here!" Marla motioned to her friend as she sat on the couch by her grandmother. "I'm just about to burst waiting to tell you both about today!"

Marla started retelling her day. Starting a new job in a new office, going shopping for office supplies, thinking that she was in a dream… Marla recounted her day with Ed, telling her story in minute detail. It would have been dull to any other listener, but it was exciting to her friends because it was something wonderful that was happening in Marla's life. They both loved her and wanted the best for her. Their smiles grew wider as they listened.

Her tone changed when she got to the part about her lunch date with Ed. Her speech slowed; and she spoke more sincerely, not like she was recalling events. Sarah saw it immediately. Her heart felt aglow. *Something happened to Marla while she was with Ed today,* Sarah thought. She settled back in her chair and waited.

"He asked me out to lunch," Marla said slowly as she gathered her thoughts. Marla was with the two people she loved most, and she wanted to tell them.

"It was just lunch. He just wanted time for us to talk. I've got so much to learn. I know nothing about the insurance business," Marla stated.

Sarah could read between the lines. Ed could have talked to Marla in the office. Sarah, as well, was captivated. She felt her joy for Marla growing with every word. For one of the few times in Sarah's life, she felt compelled to remain silent.

"We went to the golf course grill. I told the cook I'd heard about it. It's a beautiful place. I met the cook, Bart. He's adorable," Marla went on.

Bart? Adorable? Gimme a break, Marla, Sarah thought. *Gruff, loveable, funny, a good man, really…but adorable?* She knew Marla's mind had been focused on someone else.

"We went in and sat by the window. It's such a beautiful view. The golf course is lovely, so green. I loved the trees and landscaping. There seemed to be birds everywhere outside. I liked it," Marla said calmly.

Marla started in again. There was a look of joy on her face that Sarah had not noticed before, but she understood it. Sarah knew joy when she saw it. Marla was thinking about what had happened to her and how amazing it was.

"We had a pleasant lunch. Just a hamburger and fries. I think it was the best burger and fries I've ever had. It must've been Bart's cooking. Ed said he makes good hamburgers. It must've been Bart. We'll have to go there sometime, Sarah."

Sarah was mum. *You'll not like one of Bart's hamburgers as much with me*, she thought.

Marla continued, "We both talked about our lives and pasts. I liked listening to him talk."

Sarah listened as her friend's voice slowly softened and became reflective. Marla did not recognize any difference in the way she talked, but something had spoken to her heart today. Sarah could hardly keep quiet, but she would. This was her friend's moment.

Marla talked for a few more minutes and then stopped. She looked directly at Sarah. "Are you okay? You haven't spoken a word since I started talking. Are you feeling okay?"

Sarah, with a tear running down her face, said, "I've never felt better in my life. As a matter of fact, I'm feeling so good I think I want to go home and lie down."

"Sarah, sometimes I don't know what to think of you. I thought you would like to hear about my day," Marla said.

"You told me more about your day than you know. I'm so happy for you! I'm at a loss for words. Does that tell you how I feel?" Sarah stated, trying to maintain her composure.

"Well, I had a good day," Marla said with a puzzled look on her face.

"I know. And we'll talk much more about it tomorrow. Thank you for sharing it with me. Right now, I just want to go home and think about your good day. It makes me feel good. Good night, you two!" Sarah said as she hurried out the back door.

"Is she okay?" Marla asked her grandmother.

"She's fine, Dear," Emma assured her, knowing full well what had just transpired. She was as happy as Sarah. "Let's go fix some dinner. We've had a long day." Emma got up from the couch and went into the kitchen.

11

THE GIRLFRIENDS SPENT the next day working out a new routine for their many church and charity duties so that they could continue them all and leave time just to spend with each other. Then Marla would have enough time to spend at the office. Ed was completely understanding, and they all wanted God and his work to come first in their lives. And then the rest could follow.

Ed was just elated now that he had Marla in the office to take care of all the paperwork. She was a quick learner; and after they had copied all of Ed's files onto her computer, they could get the work done by communicating through text and email. At least now with the answering machine, Ed had a way for his clients to contact him. He and Marla had worked out a schedule wherein one of them was in the office about half the hours in a workweek. He had a business and could not have been happier. She had a job and felt like she was contributing in more ways now.

Sarah was just as happy and couldn't wait to talk to Marla after each work day. She was mostly interested in knowing if Marla and Ed had been together in the office.

Each time Marla was supposed to be in the office, Ed managed his schedule so he would be there too. It needed to be that way since you can only communicate so much through a cell phone. They both looked forward to those times, and the conversations weren't completely about business.

They were slowly learning more about each other; and the more they learned, the more they liked. They each saw something in the other that they'd never found in anyone else. Ed managed to find time to take Marla to lunch as often as was possible during the first few weeks. He'd even started sitting with the three women in church.

Their lives had changed for the better since that first day when Marla had arrived in Waterloo. They even felt an energy that they had never felt before. Even Emma seemed to have a new spring in her step.

Sarah was also continually talking to Marla about the ways in which a Christian should live and how Jesus should show in her life. It was evident to all who knew Marla that she was growing in her walk with God. And Marla felt it in her heart. Happiness was not as important now. She had found something profoundly better: a deep, abiding joy.

12

I T WAS A beautiful summer day. There was just enough breeze in the air to moderate the heat. The grass was still green, and the color of the trees was refreshing. It was the kind of weather that made anyone want to be outside. And that's where Sarah and Marla were that Sunday afternoon, sitting on Emma's back porch swing.

Ed had taken the three friends out to lunch in Laurens. It had been a delightful day so far for all concerned, especially for Marla. This had been the first time she had shared Ed's company with Sarah and Emma. She'd just felt so blessed today and had actually talked more than Sarah did. Marla thought that this had to have been one of the best days of her life.

"You really seemed to enjoy your lunch today," Sarah commented.

"I like Mexican food, and I'm glad we went there," Marla said.

"I liked it too," Sarah replied. "That was nice of Ed to take us all out. You know, I don't think that you, Emma, and I have ever been out to eat together. It never occurred to me until now! Yes, it was a special day. I liked the way you and Ed smile when you look at each other. You two are becoming quite a couple."

"Sarah, we are not a couple! We just work together and go to the same church, and we are involved in church activities together. And we go to Bible study together, and he comes over and talks with us, and we have lunch together sometimes. And occasionally, he will stop by the house. And we talk on the phone sometimes. That does *not* make us a couple!" Marla stated emphatically.

"Well, he's not a second cousin twice removed that no one wants either," Sarah said. "Marla, something wonderful is happening in your life.

49

Once again, she took the wind out of my sails, Marla thought. She remembered back to that day when she had asked, "Will you teach me?"

I never asked her what I wanted her to teach me, nor did I ask her to be my friend. She just said yes. Oh, God, I love that woman. Thank you for bringing such a sweet and unselfish friend into my life, Marla prayed in her head.

They stopped talking and just reflected a little on the conversation and enjoyed their time together. Each sat in her own world. Two close friends whom God had brought together.

"Marla, before I forget, I need you to take me for a doctor's appointment this Thursday in Greenville. It's an hour away. I don't think you've been there, have you?" Sarah asked.

Her friend looked up, surprised. "Why are you going to a doctor? You're as healthy as anyone else your age," she said.

Sarah hesitated. "Oh, it's just a routine follow-up. I have one every six months. My last one was the week before you got here. I had a tumor removed four years ago. They said they felt sure they had gotten all of it. The doctor just wants me to come back every six months. If it doesn't reoccur for five years, they consider you cured. It's just routine, Marla. I've been doing this. There's nothing to worry about."

Marla was concerned. Her thoughts raced, and she felt fear. "Why haven't you told me about this?"

"Marla," her friend stated calmly again, "it's okay. Just routine. They do blood work, and we come home. We can have a nice day. Greenville is a large city. There are lots of restaurants and shops. We can spend the day shopping. I'll turn you loose. You have a job and have money coming in! I think it's time you indulged in some nice clothes. *New* clothes, not that overpriced designer stuff that you used to buy. You want to look nice for Ed."

Marla calmed down. The initial shock was over. "I just wish I had known," Marla said.

"Have you told me everything that happened in your life for the last four years? No. This was just a past event. Forget about it, and let's look forward to a girl's day out in the big city. You can pay for everything," Sarah said with a big grin on her face.

13

THURSDAY CAME, AND they were both looking forward to the day in Greenville. Marla hadn't been to a large city since she arrived in Waterloo. She would be back in her former environment, to the hustle and bustle of city life. She was eager. But she still couldn't get the medical appointment out of her thoughts.

Mixed emotions made it hard for her to think as she was getting ready to go. The what-ifs kept popping up. She had to keep focusing on what Sarah had been teaching her over the past months. *God's in control. Trust him...* Marla knew that she needed to keep repeating that over and over in her mind today. And she did.

Sarah's appointment was midafternoon, so they left early and decided to spend the morning and lunchtime just being two girls out on a day of shopping. Neither one of them had ever had such excitement over a shopping trip before. It was a grand event. They found plenty of places to shop. They had fun discussing styles and prices—Marla discussed styles, and Sarah discussed prices. They made sure that each of them found a cute outfit, and they bought things for Emma, knowing it would be better than Christmas for her.

They went to the finest restaurant in town. Sarah had never been to such a place. There were white tablecloths, white linen napkins, and a highly trained waitstaff. Sarah complained about the high price of every item. "I can't believe people pay this much for food," she kept repeating. After a few bites, she did admit that it was the best-tasting food she had ever eaten but that it was still too expensive.

Marla was enjoying every minute. She had been to similar places many times before, but she realized that not one had ever been as enjoyable as this. After the crème brûlée, Sarah told her friend she could bring her back here anytime as long as Marla paid for it. After lunch, they hit the stores again. But even Marla said that they should consider just looking and not buying so much.

Soon they realized that the day had slipped by, and it was time to go back for Sarah's appointment. Her doctor's office was in a large medical complex. They parked in a handicap space by the front, and Marla wheeled Sarah in.

She was chattering away as usual, but the words did not register with Marla. She could feel anxiety rolling off of her, and her thoughts were on her friend. Marla had never experienced anything like this. Her parents were here one minute and gone the next. That was hard—very hard. She remembered. But she didn't have time before they died to feel the emotions that she was feeling now. Usually in control, she was experiencing great concern for her friend and for herself. They went into the doctor's office, signed in, and waited.

When the nurse called for Sarah, Marla took a deep breath and pushed the chair with her friend into the exam room to learn the news.

"Hello, Sarah. How are you today?" the nurse asked casually.

"Fine," Sarah said. "I like your hair. You've cut it since I was here last."

"I can't believe you would notice that, Sarah," the nurse said, smiling at the flattery of being remembered and noticed.

"She notices more than most people I know," Marla stated. "I'm Marla. I'm"—she paused for a second—"her best friend." There was a note of pride in her voice.

"That, she is," Sarah stated.

In the examination room, the nurse took vitals, updated information, and asked the usual questions. Then she rose and said, "The doctor will be in shortly." Immediately, she left the room.

Sarah just being Sarah started talking about the pictures and decor of the room, limited as it was, as if she were at a friend's house for afternoon tea. Marla was speechless, and her chest felt tight.

The doctor walked into the room. "Hello, Sarah," he said.

"Hi, Dr. Morgan," Sarah greeted back. Looking at Marla, she said, "This is Marla, my best friend, and I want her with me."

"Fine," the doctor said. "I always encourage my patients to bring a trusted companion with them."

Sarah and Dr. Morgan engaged in the usual doctor-patient dialogue: He asked how she had been feeling. She said that she was fine; that there may have been a little indigestion every now and then, but it was nothing to worry about. He entered all she said into her computer file. Sarah stayed on subject and did not discuss any of the personal things in her life since she had last seen him.

After ten minutes, the exchange was concluded, and the doctor said that all looked well. He would write an order for routine blood work, like they had done before. They could have it done down the hall. The girls had, had so much fun that day that they forgot that Sarah should not have eaten. Dr. Morgan said that it was not a problem. She could have it done tomorrow at the Laurens County Hospital, which was close to home. The results would be forwarded to his office.

After exchanging the usual pleasantries, the young women left the office and proceeded down to the car. As Marla was helping Sarah into the car, Sarah, grinning, looked up at her friend and said, "See, that wasn't as bad as you made it out to be, was it?"

Marla blushed. "Nothing perturbs me more than your being right all the time. Now, just buckle up so we can get home."

Mumbling, she closed the door while Sarah sat in the seat laughing to herself. The air in the car on the ride home was light and refreshing. The two girls had, had a great day; and that's what the conversation was on. Shopping, buying, talking, shopping, lunching, being with each other… It truly had been a girl's day out. Such a day as neither of them had enjoyed so much before. It was a day to remember.

The next days were busy. Sarah bounced from event to event, constantly engaging people in conversation on whatever her mind could conceive. Like always, her listeners were captivated and privileged for being there. The people who had witnessed the joy in her life were blessed by her presence. Sarah was something else.

Marla was with her friend everywhere when she was not at Ed's office. She loved being with and watching Sarah be Sarah. They were growing closer each day.

The next day, the three women were gathered in the living room for their morning Bible study. Sarah had chosen to read from the book of Hebrews. She knew that chapter 11 was a divinely appropriate lesson for today.

"Marla, I want you to listen carefully to this reading. This chapter is about faith. The first verse is one of the most important in the Bible. 'Now faith is being sure of what we hope for and certain of what we do not see.' Twenty-one times the writer begins a sentence with the two words *by faith*. The beginning point of faith is believing in God's character and in his promises. He is who he is, and he will do what he says."

The Bible lesson continued with Sarah's reading chapter 11 aloud.

After Bible study that morning, Sarah announced that Dr. Morgan had called and that he wanted her to come back in for a CAT scan. Marla was visually upset. Sarah tried to calm her friend, but they were like oil and water. Sarah's calm demeanor and Marla's anxiety did not blend well. Marla knew it was something bad, and she was starting to get that feeling that most people get in such a situation; she was just plain scared. The CAT scan was scheduled in two days, and Marla did not know how she would get through the time between now and then.

"What are we going to do?" Marla asked. Anxiety was written all over her face. "We have to do something."

"Wrong, Marla," Sarah said, bluntly. "God's in control. You are not. Instead of talking, you should be praying."

"I don't know how to pray like you and Ed," Marla said sadly.

"Yes, you do. You talk to God just like you are talking to me right now. Tell him how you feel. Tell him you need his help. You need his council. I still have work to do. If you want to sit here in self-absorbed self-pity, you will have to do it without me," Sarah stated firmly.

Then Sarah's demeanor changed, and her voice was calm. Sarah was now speaking to someone she loved and cared deeply about.

"God is testing you right now, Marla. You have done great works for God since you came here. I've watched your faith grow. But it never grows to a point, and then you say, 'Okay, I'm there.' A right relationship is based on faith. If you worry, doubt, and try to control the situation, then your faith is weak. And therefore, your relationship with God is weak.

"You need to work with God through this with your head held high, trusting that he has a plan for you. God's ways are not our ways. His plans are not our plans. And he doesn't need our advice. He is doing this for a purpose. Hardships often prepare ordinary people for an extraordinary destiny."

Sarah continued, now as the teacher that Marla had asked her to be.

"I believe the best book in the Bible for you now is the book of Joshua. The key to Joshua's success was his submission to God. Joshua was committed to obeying God, and this book is about obedience. He knew there was no quick solution to the problems he faced as the leader of Israel. When he led the people across the Jordan River, into the land God had promised their ancestors, it meant they were crossing from one level of faith to a new level of faith.

"Our faith grows stronger when we face obstacles. We all have our own Jericho that stands in the way of our spiritual growth. The entire book of Joshua illustrates God's faithfulness. I want you to read this book and find me passages that express Joshua's faith in God. Now, I insist that you go to the office and take care of Ed's business. I'm going to do the same with my projects. I'll have no part of worrying. We'll talk more about it this evening. But first, let's pray."

They held hands and bowed their heads. Sarah closed her eyes and spoke softly, sincerely.

"Dear Father, you have blessed us in so many ways. Thank you for our friendship, Marla's and mine. If it is your will, we pray that you will send us each your peace which passes all understanding. We ask this in Christ's name, Amen."

They sat quietly for a while, their eyes closed, heads bowed, and hands clasped. Each prayed silently in her own heart. Then Marla left for the office feeling a new calm and confidence. When Ed arrived, she told him what had happened and all that Sarah had told her. Ed was sorry and said that he would pray for her.

"Marla, let's sit down. Jesus taught many lessons on worrying. Each one was '*Don't do it!* It'll accomplish nothing.' Worry does not take away tomorrow's trouble, but it takes away today's peace. There's not enough room in your mind for both worry and faith. You have to decide which one will live there. What we have to do today can wait for a while. Get out your Bible, and we'll find those passages. I want to help you and Sarah through this. I'll be with you, Marla."

Feeling a tightness in her throat, she reached out, put her arms around Ed, and hugged him firmly and lovingly. Then she said, "I'm not sorry I did that this time."

"I'm even more glad you did it this time. Do it again anytime you feel you need a hug," Ed said, looking deeply into her eyes.

Marla realized she now had three teachers: Sarah, Ed, and the Holy Spirit. Ed believed that God was in control, just like Sarah did.

Then it hit her. These two people, she could admit to herself and herself only, she loved. *They're speaking the same message. That's the common link between these two*, Marla thought. *It's God!* The light that had been born in her and had been growing in her was now making her aware of its presence. God was revealing himself to Marla. She could dispute other messages from her previous life but not this one.

Ed started speaking again, "Your friend may be facing a profound life experience. You'll regret it for the rest of your life if you don't do what she wishes. She only wants the best for you. If you love her, start acting like it. Be strong. You are not the only one who cares about Sarah. This whole town will be sad when they know what's happening. Sarah is a friend to everyone here."

14

SARAH WAS SITTING with Emma in the living room when Marla walked in from work. Her heart almost broke when she saw Sarah; and she immediately ran to her, leaned over, and hugged her so hard that it startled Sarah.

"Not so hard, Marla. I don't want to have to go a chiropractor too," Sarah said with a smile on her face.

"I love you, Sarah," Marla said plainly. "I'm sorry for the way I acted earlier. I got a repeat of what you said from Ed at the office. God is in control."

Emma chuckled, never missing anything between the young women. She loved her two granddaughters.

"Here's my homework assignment," Marla stated. "Four times in chapter 1, God tells Joshua to 'Be strong and courageous.' And God said, 'Do not be discouraged, the Lord your God will be with you wherever you go. I will never leave you nor forsake you.' I need to be strong like Joshua.

"Joshua conquered all the lands and destroyed all his enemies with the help of God. But God did this for Joshua because he trusted God completely. God could have simply destroyed Jericho by his will, but the army of Joshua did it by following the orders God gave Joshua. I need to trust in God like Joshua did.

"The conquest of the lands fulfilled God's promise to Israel that he gave to their forefathers. His promises, whatever they are, will be fulfilled by *his* timetable, not ours. I should faithfully do what I know he wants me to do and trust him for the future like Joshua did."

Finally, Marla concluded, "I need to live as Joshua did when he stated in chapter 24, verse 15, 'But as for me and my household, we will serve the Lord.'"

"Well done!" Sarah said, beaming with joy. She was proud of her student.

"Sarah, I promise I'll always cherish and enjoy our relationship, whatever God has planned for us."

That did it. All three women started weeping.

On the day of the CAT scan, the two friends had a conversation on the way to the hospital. Sarah was chattering away while Marla was listening to every word, cherishing the moment. Something had happened to Marla. She had a sense of calm that she had not felt before. It was like the burden of concern about what to do had been removed. *No, I have just given it to someone else*, she thought. Someone had spoken to her heart and said, "Give it to me. I'll deal with it for you." And she knew that, that is exactly what had occurred.

It was 8:00 a.m. when they arrived at the outpatient wing of the medical complex building. Marla took Sarah in, and they began filling out the necessary paperwork. Sarah had followed the instructions given to her prior to coming and was ready.

When they took her friend in for the CAT scan, Marla felt like something inside her was missing as she sat by herself. She'd never been sick or had physical problems. She had rarely been in a doctor's office other than for routine checkups until her visit to Dr. Morgan with Sarah. And she didn't like the feeling she had in this place. But she knew what to do. She closed her eyes and talked to God. It felt good. Then she didn't feel alone.

"God, whatever happens, I'll trust you. I'm new at this, but I know you and Sarah are not," she prayed silently.

She went over to the magazine rack, not giving *Vogue* a second glance but reaching for *The Upper Room*. Upon seeing the subtitle "Where the World Meets to Pray," she took the magazine. Her eyes were drawn to an article entitled, "Signs." The scripture under the title said, "Trust in the Lord with all your heart and lean not on your own understanding." Proverbs 3:5. The short essay was about learning to ignore negative signs. The prayer at the end went, "Dear God, help us to trust in you and rejoice in the journeys of our lives. Help us to let go of negative thoughts so we can follow you."

Marla felt a sensation that she'd never experienced before. This magazine was filled with lessons, she realized. But this one spoke directly to her. She stopped reading, amazed. *My Lord, you just spoke to me, didn't you?*

She put the magazine down and tried to regain her composure. A sense of elation came over Marla. She thought back to the first morning Bible reading with her grandmother and Sarah. She remembered how Sarah had spoken so plainly to her about the wonders of God, how God wanted the best for her, and how Marla had asked her new friend to teach her. She remembered thinking that her relationship with Sarah had taken a new turn.

Oh, God, Marla thought, *Sarah was right. Sarah was so often right.* And now Marla knew her relationship with God had taken a new turn too, and she knew why. She had trusted in God, given herself over to God; and God had given back to her. The seed that had been planted so long ago, when her parents had taken her to church, had sprouted. God had caused it to grow in her. The old Marla, the one from Chicago—glamorous and worldly—was gone.

The nurse brought Sarah back into the waiting room.

"We're all done," she said to Marla. "You can take her home now. The doctor will call Sarah when he has the results. Tomorrow, at the latest." The nurse turned and walked away.

Sarah had not taken her eyes off Marla. Sarah hadn't even spoken to the nurse. Marla had a familiar look on her face. It reminded Sarah of her friend's expression after the first lunch with Ed. Sarah knew something exciting and wonderful had happened in Ed and Marla's relationship. Sarah thought, *I'm seeing the same thing now. The excitement, the wonder... I think I'll do what I did then. I'll be quiet and listen. Marla wants to tell me something.*

Her friend looked at Sarah and smiled. "Well, how did it go?"

"Oh, fine. I just lay there for a while as this machine did its thing, and now here I am," Sarah said matter-of-factly. "How did it go with you?"

There was a long pause, and Sarah had to bite her tongue to keep from talking.

"Something ha—happened to me," Marla stammered, "and it was kind of amazing. Let's get out of here! I don't want to talk about it in here."

"Okay, let's go," Sarah said. She wasn't concerned. Whatever had happened, she could tell by the look on Marla's face that it had been stunning.

Marla hurried the two of them out of the building and into her car. She helped Sarah in, put the wheelchair in the back, and slid into the driver's seat. Marla just sat there gazing out of the windshield. Sarah waited and then said, "Uh, Marla, the car won't move until you turn on the ignition."

Marla snapped out of it. "Sarah, I think maybe God spoke to me while I was in the waiting room. I didn't hear his voice, but I think I felt his voice." Marla then proceeded to tell Sarah in detail every second of what had transpired while Sarah was having her scan. Sarah listened thoughtfully to every word as she studied her friend's thoughtful and radiant face.

Perhaps Marla's fruitless search for happiness had been replaced by a supply of something with never-ending joy and hope. The joy that only comes from a personal relationship with God. Marla had it now. Marla had it all. She had the belief in and love of God, the love of Sarah, the love of her grandmother, and, she remembered, the love of Ed. She was glowing and full of hope.

Marla drove home, jabbering all the way. The love was pouring out of her for the first time in their friendship, and Sarah could not get a word in edgewise. Marla was doing all the talking. *What a change has come over my friend*, Sarah thought.

15

THE NEXT MORNING, Sarah received a call from Dr. Morgan. "Sarah, I've got some bad news. The CAT scan we took of your abdomen and pelvis showed what the radiologist feels are clear signs. I think you have ovarian cancer, and it has metastasized into your pelvic region. I think the best thing right now is surgery to remove the ovaries and maybe other parts of your reproductive organs. We won't know until we go in and see how far the cancer has advanced. Then you will need to undergo chemotherapy.

"Sarah, I can't give you any prognosis at this time. We need to do more tests, and the surgery will tell us more. I feel we need to get started on this as soon as possible. Can we schedule the surgery for the first available date after we have run the preliminary tests and biopsies?"

Sarah was silent, and tears formed in her eyes. Then her practical voice responded, "Yes, Doctor. Tell me what I need to do, and let's get started."

The doctor said, "I'll have my office schedule the necessary tests and call you later today to discuss scheduling all this. We need to move as quickly as possible. Sarah, I'm so sorry to have to tell you this. It's the part of my profession that I don't like. Nothing makes it easier."

"Dr. Morgan, I know that's what it is. I'm a child of God, and I'll deal with what is handed to me. I know you'll do the best you can for me."

"That you can depend on," Dr. Morgan stated. Then he hung up the phone.

Sarah took several deep breaths. Closing her eyes, she said a silent prayer. Then she said to herself, "I need to get busy. I have laundry in the washer that needs to be put into the drier. I need to pay the bills that are due. I need to pack for the hospital stay that I know is coming. I have so many commitments coming up that I need to get someone else to cover for me."

A dozen things crossed her mind, and they were all about others. That was Sarah. Plain and practical. And unselfish. Now Sarah knew that the next step was going to be hard. She had to tell Marla and Emma, and it had to be done immediately. Sarah knew that Marla had gone to the office, but Emma would be home. So she called Marla.

"Hi, Sarah," Marla answered.

"I don't like having to tell you this, but Dr. Morgan called and said the tests showed what they feel are signs of cancer. I need to talk to you and Emma about it this morning because he wants me to have surgery as soon as possible. He's scheduling tests, and I'll need your help."

"O—okay, Sarah," Marla stammered. "I'll come home now."

She had met God, and his essence was interwoven in her life. But now she wondered if the strand was broken. What was, was never to be the same again. Marla's new life, which had begun when she came to Waterloo, seemed to have ended. *God, what are you doing? You spoke to me. I listened. I understood. I thought we had a relationship. Why this, Lord? What did I miss?*

"Trust in God," she kept saying to herself. But now the severity of Sarah's cancer had been made real. Sarah had a life-threatening situation. Marla knew that she would have to harness all that she had within her to get through this. Then it hit her. *This isn't about me. This is about Sarah.* Marla hated herself for her thoughts. Upon realizing this, she resolved to pray: "God, give me the strength."

Marla quickly ended her work at the office. At home, she found Sarah sitting on the couch with Emma. It was obvious that Sarah had already told Emma, who was weeping as Sarah consoled her. Marla put her arms around Sarah, hugging her compassionately and starting to cry as well. Sarah responded in kind. After a while, the three of them regained their composure. Sarah spoke first.

"Okay, look, you two… I need you both to be strong for me. I have a lot to do and a very short time to do it. When Dr. Morgan's office calls, I need to be ready to go and do what they need done as far as the preliminary tests go. Then I'll probably have to go very soon after into the hospital.

"The doctor said it looks like ovarian cancer, and it may have spread into my pelvic region. He said I need surgery as soon as possible. They'll go in and remove parts that are malignant. I'll have to have chemo after that. This is going to occupy my time for a while until I can come back home. I have to arrange for people to take care of all the things I help with. There are people who need and want my help. I can't just leave all that—"

Marla interrupted, "Stop it. Stop right there, Sarah." She said this with such authority that it caught both Sarah and Emma off guard.

"Look, Sister, this is how it's going to be. For the first time in your life here in Waterloo, you are not going to think about other people. You have a problem, and you and I and Emma are going to deal with it. But the focus is going to be on Sarah. God is in charge, but he cannot and will not do everything for us. We have a responsibility in his plan for us, and we have to do our part. Sarah, I'll walk every step with you. I'll fight tigers for you, if necessary. But you need to focus on helping yourself and no one else for a change."

For the first time in their relationship, Marla had taken the wind out of Sarah's sails. She felt like she had forgotten how to speak. Emma jumped right in where Marla had stopped.

"She's right, Sarah. I know everything you do, who you do it for, and who you do it with. You have a loving, caring church family, and any of them would wring your neck if you didn't permit them to help you now. I'm going to start making phone calls right now. You two go over to Sarah's house and start packing and getting her house ready for her to leave for a while. Sarah, you're no longer in charge. Now, you two, get out of here. I have work to do."

Marla started back in again. "Sarah, you go over to your house and get started. Ed is at the office waiting for me. I told him what you said before I left the office. I want to tell him in person what we have discussed now. I'm going to go back there and then will come to your house and help you."

Emma picked up the phone and started dialing. Marla turned and walked out the door.

With sloth-like slowness, Sarah turned her motorized scooter chair and made her way out of Emma's back door and over to her house, thinking as she went. Sarah had, had a hard life. She knew it, but she just didn't let it show. She had a physical handicap that would have caused a lot of people to just sit down in a chair and watch the days fly by.

Sarah had made up her mind a long time ago that she wouldn't let that happen to herself. She always lived by what the Apostle Paul wrote in his letter to the Philippians: "Let this mind be in you which was in Christ Jesus." That's the mind of a servant. That's why she never stopped. She only had two speeds: fast and off. She had long ago learned that adversity is a challenge, not an obstacle. But now, for the first time in her adult life, she was not making the decisions about her life. She felt uncertain yet about a hundred times more loved beyond measure.

As she reached her house, she began organizing her thoughts so that she and Marla could take care of what needed to be done when her friend returned.

At the office, it was obvious to Ed that Marla had been crying. They walked toward each other and hugged, neither wanting the other to stop. After a time, Ed said, "Let's sit down on the couch. Tell me everything."

"Oh, Ed," Marla said, holding back the tears, "it's bad. She said it's ovarian cancer. She's going to have some more tests. Then she's having surgery. And she will need chemotherapy. This is all happening so fast I can't get my mind around it.

"You and Sarah have always taught me that God is in control and has a plan for us. What is his plan for Sarah? Would you explain that to me? You could search all over and not find a person who loves God and loves doing for God more than Sarah. Now God may take her away. Why, Ed? Why do bad things happen to people like Sarah?

Why does God allow tragedy and suffering?" At this, she started crying.

Ed responded, "I don't have the answer, and no one else does either. We have to accept by faith that God is sovereign, and he is a God of love and mercy and compassion in the midst of suffering. I pray that God will calm your heart and that he'll open your mind to understand what best serves the truth and the lives of those involved. Marla, people have been asking *why* for thousands of years. Job asked *why*. The writers of Psalms asked *why*. We witnessed two world wars and the Holocaust, and people asked *why*."

Ed went into his office and returned looking through his Bible.

"Here it is," he said. "John 16:33. Jesus speaking, 'You will have suffering in this world.' He did not say you *might* have it. He said it's *going* to happen. And he said, 'In him you will find peace.'

"Marla, I'm going to be right there with you, helping you through this. Sarah will need your help. She can't go through this alone. Everyone in church will be available. I doubt you could get fewer than a hundred people to help. But Sarah needs Marla beside her. And, Marla, I'll be beside you. Don't worry about the office. I have a place to work now that you have it running the way I wanted. I know you love Sarah. I just want you to know... I love you."

She had already started to have feelings for him. Looking into Ed's face and eyes, she saw his love for her. The joy welling up within her was incredible. But Marla knew love. It was in every breath she'd taken and with everyone she met with who loved her since she arrived in Waterloo. She put her arms around Ed's neck and kissed him on the lips. Ed returned the kiss.

"I love you, Ed," Marla said.

"I love you too," Ed responded.

She did not want this moment to end. But she knew Sarah was waiting and needed her. She looked up at Ed.

"Sarah's waiting for me. I need to go help her," Marla said, her face aglow.

"I know," Ed replied. "I'll stop by this evening and see you two."

16

E D ARRIVED AT Emma's house at about six thirty that evening. Marla, Sarah, and Emma were all together discussing the arrangements that Emma had made with everyone. Ed was right—it seems there were a hundred people from church involved. The kitchen table was already piled with food, and the refrigerator was full.

Half a dozen ladies from church had been buzzing around Sarah's house, getting things done. Mrs. Rodriguez had come over to clean and vacuum when they were all through. So now they were just preparing for tomorrow. Dr. Morgan's office had called; and he informed Sarah that tests were scheduled for the next day, starting with an exam and consultation with him first thing in the morning.

Ed walked over to Marla, kissed her on the cheek, and sat down. "You girls keep on with what you're doing. I'll just sit here and listen to the plans," Ed said.

Sarah and Emma looked at Marla briefly as Ed kissed her; then, they looked at each other and smiled. They both knew what had been going on between Ed and Marla. This just validated it for them. For a moment, the cares of the problem with Sarah had been replaced with joy in their hearts for the love that had come into Marla's life.

Marla picked up where the conversation had stopped when Ed came in.

"Well, I think that about covers it. Sarah, we need to leave early, so let's all turn in early. You have so many people that love you and care about you. Please try and get some sleep tonight. God is in control, along with a whole bunch of people here in Waterloo. Isn't that right, Ed?" Marla asked, turning her head and looking at him, smiling.

"You got that right, Marla," Ed replied. The look on his face spoke volumes to Sarah and Emma. Their joy and love for Marla at the moment made them forget the reality of the day.

Sarah and Emma shared the same thought. Sarah spoke it. "Well, then, since there's nothing more to discuss—and since you are always right, Marla—Emma and I'll turn in early. It's going to be a long day tomorrow, isn't it, Emma? I want to take a shower and read my Bible in bed for a while, and then get a good night's sleep. Thank you both for all you've done today."

"I feel the same way, Sarah. I haven't made so many phone calls in one day in my entire life! But each person I spoke to was so happy to lend a hand. Sarah, you have dozens of brothers and sisters here. Sweet dreams, Dear," Emma said affectionately.

"Same to you, Emma," Sarah said.

The women started to leave; and they both spoke at the same time, looking at Marla and Ed.

"You two have a nice evening."

When they had left, Ed asked, "What was that all about? Is everything okay with the plans for what you and Sarah have to do?"

"Yes," answered Marla. "We've been sitting here for an hour talking and have planned as much as we can. So many ladies from the church and some from the community have been over to help or to offer to help, or they have brought food. It's amazing to me how the word spread so fast, and so many people want to help."

Ed answered calmly, "Sarah is part of a church family, and that's what family does for a member in need."

"I have an inner calm that I wouldn't have thought possible months ago in a situation like this. I love it," Marla stated.

"Marla," Ed interjected, "I think you are learning about God's *agape* love. It's not what the world thinks or understands about love. Sarah has always had it. Her love for others was always about what she could do for them, what she could give to others."

Marla had always seen this in Sarah. This is what she wondered about the first time they met. She found herself thinking about *agape* love. God was shining a light into Marla's heart; and she saw that light, that love of others, reflected. She saw the same *agape* love in

Emma and in Ed. She'd seen it in the people who had come over today to offer their help. It was a love expressed in giving to and helping others.

Oh, Marla, she thought, *how could you not notice what was so obvious to everyone?* She knew the answer. It was because she didn't possess what they possessed. She saw it now clearly.

Her thoughts returned to the moment, and she realized that she and Ed were alone. She had been deep in thought, and Ed hadn't said a word.

She broke the silence. "I'm sorry, Ed. I was somewhere else."

"Marla, I knew where you were," Ed said. "I don't know what you were thinking, but I was there with you."

He reached over and hugged Marla firmly so there would be no mistake of the motive. It was purely out of caring. Marla could feel it, and she understood it. They sat on the couch and talked for a long time.

17

T HE WOMEN ARRIVED at Dr. Morgan's office first thing
the next morning. They both knew that the doctor had
changed his appointments to get Sarah in first, and they both
knew what that meant. They completed the usual paperwork, and
the nurse took them in from the waiting room. Today, it was just a
simple exchange between them on the way to the exam room. The
friends sat silently, each reflecting on her own thoughts.

Dr. Morgan opened the door, entered, and sat down in his
chair. "How are you feeling today, Sarah?" he asked.

"Okay, I guess. How *should* I feel today?" she asked.

He chuckled. "You are a very special woman, Sarah. Forgive
me."

"That's okay, Doctor," she said sincerely.

"We'll start with a complete physical exam this morning. I need
to know what's going on with your body and be sure you are phys-
ically able to undergo surgery. You understand?" the doctor asked.

"Yes," she replied.

"Then I've scheduled an ultrasound and a bone marrow biopsy.
The ultrasound will show us what is happening in your body, and the
biopsy will show whether the cancer has spread to the bone marrow."
Then he looked at Marla. "Marla. It is Marla, isn't it?"

"Yes," Marla replied.

"I need you to wait outside, and I'll call you in when it's time."

"Okay," she said as she rose from her chair. She then reached
over to her friend with a hug and a kiss on the cheek.

Sarah looked at her companion with love and apprehension.
She whispered softly and slowly, "Don't worry."

Marla responded in kind, "I won't."

She headed back into the waiting room. There were a few people there. Wanting to be alone, Marla found a chair away from the others. *This is the time you provided for me, isn't it, God?* She prayed silently. She thought of Sarah, Emma, Ed, and all the people in the church and the community. *Oh, God, how you've blessed me so. I never dreamed in all my life that I would have loving, caring friends such as I have now.*

But more than that, she had a relationship that transcended all of these. Marla had found the fountain of life, the living water. "Drink of me and never be thirsty again."

Marla, she thought, *you are facing the greatest crisis so far in your life. The best person and friend ever to come into your life—oh, God, there's the possibility that you may take her back to be with you...* Marla faced the situation, the possibility of Sarah's death, but with God beside her. Still, it was a human event and had to be faced with human emotions. Then she remembered that Jesus had been human and had felt human emotions too.

So God knows exactly what I feel because he felt it too. Jesus wept at the death of his friend Lazarus. God knows how I feel now, but that does not take away the heartache I feel. Oh, God, my heart's breaking for Sarah and what she's going to have to go through. Lord, I love you, but I have to confess. I don't know what I should feel, what I should think, what I should do. Lord, what is next? Marla asked silently.

She anticipated some response or feeling. But there was only silence. Not just in the room but in her heart as well. She felt alone. The room was still and so cold. She kept waiting, but nothing happened. No answer came.

Where are you, God, she wondered? *You have been speaking to me. Where are you?*

"Marla. Marla!"

Looking to the waiting-room door, she saw the nurse standing in the doorway, looking a little impatient.

Marla snapped back from her thoughts. "I'm coming! Sorry," she said as she hurried through the door.

"Come this way," the nurse said. They went into a room where Sarah was sitting in a chair, looking calm.

"How are you doing?" Sarah asked.

"Okay," Marla responded with a faint smile.

"Oh, come on, Marla! I know it's no fun sitting and waiting, rereading all those old magazines!" she answered, with a knowing twinkle in her eyes.

"Sarah, if I live to be a hundred years old, I'll forever be amazed at you," Marla said, smiling back at her friend.

Marla was so glad to see that her friend was again making light of things. She was so often surprised at Sarah's great spirit of fun. *Always an example for me. And I'm always watching and learning,* Marla reflected.

"Will you please tell me what the doctor said?" Marla asked, with a serious look on her face.

Sarah understood. "I'm healthy enough for surgery, so that will proceed as planned. They want to do a bone biopsy shortly because if the cancer has spread to the bone marrow, that means it's widespread. I have to have more blood work done, so the vampires get to draw more blood out of me. Then I go in for an ultrasound. Then we can go home. Where are you taking us for dinner? I don't want to eat church casserole tonight."

Marla wondered, *Who needs Valium when you can be with Sarah? If a person can't feel calm and understand the essence and meaning of life when in her presence, then he is spiritually dead. Being with Sarah is a little taste of heaven. God is present when you're around her.*

Marla went to all the tests with Sarah on her mission to make everyone in her presence joyful. Marla knew better and wouldn't have wanted to stop it if she had thought for one second that she could. Sarah touched everyone she came in contact with that day, and she did so with the joy in her heart and the source of that joy shining through. All who encountered Sarah experienced her joy.

When the two girlfriends left the hospital, Sarah had lightened the burden of everyone she had met. People noticed the woman in the wheelchair being pushed down the hall at the hospital, into the elevator, and out into the parking lot. Her beautiful and sincere smile touched hearts. People smiled back, and some even turned to look again after she passed. Marla understood it. She was there watching it, and she didn't want the day to end.

As Sarah had requested, Marla drove them to that great Italian restaurant for dinner. They had a most enjoyable dinner as well as good conversation. Sarah, bubbly and effervescent; and Marla, thoughtful and admiring.

They drove home as if nothing of any particular significance had happened that day. Ed came over, and the four friends talked through the events of the day, good friends and all. It was a pleasant evening all around.

*****

The surgery was scheduled for 7:00 a.m., the day after tomorrow. Sarah was told to check into the hospital tomorrow between 12:00 p.m. and 3:00 p.m. She'd been instructed to stay home and rest until then. Dr. Morgan knew he would have to make allowances with Sarah. So he had told her to rest her body; he knew she couldn't rest her mouth, but that would be okay. Sarah chuckled when he said that.

He said that Dr. Ben Stearns had agreed to come to their hospital to perform the surgery, and she would be in the best of hands. Dr. Stearns was the best gynecologic oncologist in this part of South Carolina. He was trained and experienced in ovarian cancer and surgery. She had medicine to take at specific times and a specific diet of food and drink for the next two days and evenings. Sarah couldn't resist and stated that she would miss her three martinis this evening.

This time, it was Dr. Morgan who chuckled. He finished with "Just get a good night's sleep. We need you rested when you get to the hospital."

They exchanged goodbyes and hung up. Sarah then proceeded to tell Marla and Emma what she had been told.

Emma spoke first. "Sarah, the people in this town are beside themselves thinking about you. I have to allow some of our closest friends to come over and visit with you. They love you and want to talk to you. For a change, you are going to sit quietly and listen to people who love you tell you so."

Emma looked up for Marla's support. She didn't have to. Marla was just waiting for her cue.

"She's right. This is family Emma's talking about. Emma, start calling whoever you want over here. Just tell them they need to keep the visits short since others want to visit and Sarah needs to rest."

Looking at Sarah, Marla said, "Save your breath, Sister. We out-rank you now. Do you want something to drink before your family starts showing up?"

"A cup of tea would be lovely. Thank you," Sarah said with a joy in her heart greater than she had ever felt before.

The next six hours, Emma began to wonder if her screen door would survive the constant opening and closing. But to Emma, the sound it made each time was like a carol sung by a choir. Everyone could feel the love in the room that day. It was like the scent in the air when one is in a rose garden. And there was beauty all around. The spirit of God hovered over Emma's house.

18

SARAH AND EMMA had said their goodbyes. Marla was helping Sarah into the car after she had packed Sarah's belongings. They drove to the hospital. It was quiet in the car. Sarah knew this wasn't the time for idle chatter. Instead, she closed her eyes and prayed.

Marla tried to pray as well, but she couldn't form the words in her mind. She felt alone. She didn't know why God had been silent. Oh, she had seen the love of God expressed by all the people who had come to see Sarah. There was no mistake about that. So Marla just had to accept that God was still in control, whether he let her know about it or not.

They arrived at the hospital and went to the admitting office. They filled out more paperwork, and then a nurse's aide took Sarah to the floor where she would be staying. Marla followed, carrying Sarah's things. They went to the nurse's station. The aide then handed a file to the nurse on duty.

"Hi, Sarah. I'm Kathy. I'll be taking care of you this afternoon. We've been expecting you. I have everything ready. Are you having any problems or symptoms I should know about?"

"The only problem is I'd rather be somewhere else, but I know you can't fix that one," Sarah said casually. "I just love your red hair! It looks to me to be the natural color. Is it?"

"Yes, it is," Kathy said, smiling.

"You are really fortunate to be blessed with that. I see you have a band on your left ring finger. I assume you wear that when on duty instead of your real wedding ring so others will know you're married? Do you have any children?"

Sarah was just carrying on a conversation like she would with someone standing in line at a store. Marla realized she was shaking her head slightly from side to side as she watched Sarah be Sarah.

"I have three. Two boys and one girl," Kathy replied. Being a professional, she followed that statement up quickly with "Let's get you in your room and get you settled in. Dr. Stearns has ordered pre-surgery tests we need to get started on, and I need to get your IVs going so we can get those pre-surgery meds started. I'll take you to your room. Number 307." Then she looked at Marla. "You can follow us."

As Kathy was pushing her along, Sarah informed, "This is Marla, my best and closest friend."

"Hello, Marla," Kathy said. "I'm glad you're with her."

They entered Sarah's room.

"Sarah, I'll give you a couple of minutes to get into this hospital gown and use the bathroom now so Marla can help you. Don't eat or drink anything you may have brought. You'll be on a strict diet of food and liquid for now. Marla, I'll step outside. You let me know when Sarah is in bed." Kathy turned and walked out, pulling the door almost closed.

"Well, it's started. Let's do what she said," Sarah said.

To Marla, it was as if she were watching a movie. A movie with herself and Sarah as the characters. She was moving and talking, but it didn't seem real. When Sarah was in bed, Marla went out and found Kathy, who came into Sarah's room and began her duties. Kathy started the IV. Marla was putting Sarah's things into drawers. She put Sarah's Bible on the bedside table and sat down in the chair.

She sat there for the next few hours as people came and went, doing whatever it was that they needed to do. Marla's mind was in a fog, and she was just an observer. Sarah, however, saw this as another opportunity to converse with and share her joy with a whole new bunch of people. She was in her element, even if she was at a hospital.

Ed showed up as he had promised. When he walked in, Marla came out of her trance. She got up from the chair, met him, and hugged him tightly. "I'm so glad you're here," she said. "I feel so useless right now."

Upon hearing this, Sarah spoke up to correct her friend. "Marla, you're not useless. You're doing just what I need. You're here with me. I couldn't do this if you weren't here with me. Now, the two of you, sit down. I think all the munchkins have done everything they needed to do too. I need someone to talk to."

That brought Marla back to life. "Sarah, all you've done for the past few hours is talk." She actually laughed as she said it.

Ed sat in the chair, and Marla sat on the edge of the bed. They started having conversation, and Marla felt like herself again.

It was 6:00 p.m. when Ed said he needed to leave. Marla said she was going to stay as long as she could. She was feeling a little hungry; but however she felt, she didn't want to leave Sarah. Someone had brought in Sarah's meal earlier; and even as limited as it was, she'd eaten most of it.

Ed left, and a few minutes later, Kathy came in with another nurse.

"This is Betty," Kathy said to Sarah. "She'll be your nurse for tonight." She looked toward Marla and said, "That's her friend Marla." They nodded at each other.

"I'm going off duty soon. I've filled Betty in on everything. It's all in the doctor's orders we follow. Betty and I both have been doing this for many years. I just have to go over everything with her and confirm all the IV bags and meds I've started. You just relax for a few minutes while we take care of what we need to for a change of staff."

"I understand," Sarah said as she settled back in bed and watched and listened.

Betty and Kathy started leaving the room. "I'll be in, in just a few minutes," Betty said.

"I'll be right here," Sarah said with a smile on her face. Sarah looked at Marla. "You okay? You've been awfully quiet today."

"I'm fine, Sarah. Just a little dazed. Everything seems to be moving so fast."

"I know," Sarah said, picking up her Bible. "I think I want to read to you for both of us."

"Fine," Marla said, settling back in the chair. Sarah read for a while, and then Betty returned.

"So are you feeling okay? Any complaints other than that the food was bland, and you don't want to be here?" Betty asked with a smile on her face.

"I'm fine, and you're right about the other two," Sarah replied, returning Betty's smile.

"I just want to let you know what to expect for now until they come get you for your surgery. First, try and get what sleep you can in between the people coming and going all night. That's just the way it is. I'll be in often, checking vitals. You'll have blood drawn in a short while and then shortly before you're taken to surgery. There will be others coming in. You don't have to do anything except maybe answer a question.

"About five in the morning, someone will take you down to surgery to start prepping you. I'll have given you a mild relaxant before. Down there, they'll start you on the drugs to slowly take you out of reality. The anesthesiologist is on the floor and will be in shortly to explain all that to you. Dr. Morgan, I believe, is in the hospital making rounds, and he'll be in to see you. The best thing you can do for yourself is try to rest and sleep after the doctors have left. Do you have any questions?"

"No," Sarah replied. She knew this was real now, and it was not a laughing matter anymore.

"Marla," Betty said, looking at her, "you can stay as long as Sarah wants, but you need to leave by nine."

"I understand," Marla stated plainly. Betty left.

Sarah and Marla just looked at each other. They were both thinking how much they loved the other. No words needed to be spoken by either of them.

When 9:00 a.m. came, Marla knew that she needed to leave. The doctors had come and talked to Sarah. She understood what they said. It was all a blur to Marla. She needed to leave now because that would be the best thing for Sarah. Marla thought, *What if she dies tonight? What if she dies during surgery? What if—Stop it, Marla! Stop it!* She regained her composure.

"Sarah, I love you. I love you so much," Marla said with tears in her eyes.

"I know, Marla. I love you too," Sarah said, starting to cry too.

Marla reached down and hugged Sarah, both of them with tears. Sarah, being the practical one, said, "We both know you really need to leave."

"I know, Sarah. I just don't want to. I know I have to. I know. It's just so hard to leave you now. So hard. I feel like I'm abandoning you."

"No, I'm in good hands. You're not in control. God is. Everyone here has a job to do. The people who work in this hospital know what they have to do and how to do it. I know what I have to do. Your job is to pray and trust in God. Everyone else is doing their job. You go home and do yours."

Marla couldn't remember any instance of Sarah crying like she was now. She knew she had to leave. Standing in the doorway, she saw that smile that she knew so well return to Sarah's face.

"Sweet dreams," Sarah said softly.

"You too," Marla answered as she turned and walked out.

19

MARLA, ED, AND Emma arrived early the next morning. They notified the receptionist that they were the family of Sarah and asked where to wait for the doctor during the surgery. They were directed to the waiting room. Dr. Stearns came to talk to the family as he always does after a major surgery. Sarah had already designated Marla, Emma, and Ed as family that could have access to all information on her from her medical records. The doctor found the three of them in the surgery waiting room and asked them to follow him into a private consultation room.

"Well, the surgery went well, and she's in recovery. There are no complications from the surgery. However, as far as the cancer is concerned, it's extensive. It's metastasized into other organs in her pelvic region and possibly beyond.

"I removed all her reproductive organs because they all had signs of cancer. I removed other areas that had cancerous growth on them. I won't go into medical detail. The lab will analyze tissue and fluid samples I removed to better evaluate the type and expanse of the cancer. My report and the lab results will be forwarded to Dr. Morgan. He'll get with Sarah and you to discuss further treatment.

"At this time, I see no need for further surgery. She'll be in recovery for a while to be sure she's stable and is coming out of the anesthesia. When she's in her room and the nurse has her settled in, you'll be allowed to visit her. I suggest one of you go to the nurse's station and let them know where you'll be. They can contact you when you can see her. I wish I didn't have to tell you this. I'm sorry. Dr. Morgan is as good as there is in this area. You can have confidence in him. Do you have any questions?"

Ed looked at Marla and Emma. They had the look of a couple of deer in the headlights. Ed replied for the women, "No, thank you, Doctor."

Dr. Stearns got up and left the room.

"You two wait here. I'm going to go up to the nurse's station and give them my cell number. I'll tell them we will want to see Sarah as soon as we can," Ed said calmly.

He knew that he would have to be the rock now. Marla and Emma were going to be too emotional, and rightly so. Ed leaned over and kissed Marla. Then he took Emma's right hand and placed it between his two hands, giving it a gentle squeeze, and left the room.

Marla reached over to Emma, and they hugged each other. Neither of them could stop the tears from flowing. They stayed that way until Ed returned a few minutes later.

"Marla," Ed called. She looked up at Ed. "The nurse has my number, and she'll call me when they've brought Sarah back to the room. She said Sarah will still be feeling the effects of the sedation and will probably not be able to understand if you are here. She'll wait until Sarah is coherent then call me. She said Sarah will probably be here for a minimum of four days anyway. It's pointless for us to just sit here for no telling how many hours. I want to take you two home. I'll bring you back when it's time. Okay?"

Ed drove them home. They all went into Emma's house and sat down, emotionally exhausted and grief-stricken. Ed said a prayer out loud for the three of them and for Sarah. He said he was going into the kitchen to make a pot of tea, not knowing if anyone would want any. It was just something to do.

When Ed returned, Marla said, "Ed, call Dr. Morgan, and ask him when he'll be going to see Sarah. We can go back then, and he can talk to all of us at the same time. Tell him I don't want Sarah to hear about all this alone."

"Good idea," Ed said proudly.

Dr. Morgan had given his cell number to them, and Ed called him. The doctor agreed. He would be at the hospital between five and five thirty this evening to make rounds. Meanwhile, Ed knew that Emma had, had enough for one day, and the stress this evening would be too much for her. Marla and Emma agreed.

Ed was going to the office; but before he left, he gave the two some important instructions.

"You two get some rest. I need you both to have a clear head. Sarah's starting on a new journey, and she going to need our support. Start thinking like Sarah. Think practical."

It was like Ed had thrown a bucket of water in Marla's face. She actually had a slight smile on.

"I love you, Ed Fielding. You're exactly right." Sarah could not have said it better.

"Emma," Marla started, "your back bedroom hasn't been used for a long time. I've been thinking… Let's turn it into a bedroom for Sarah so she'll have one or both of us here all the time. We can move Sarah's bedroom from her house over here. I'm sure we'll know more what we need after we talk to Dr. Morgan this evening. I know we could get an army of church friends to help us."

"You're exactly right, Marla. It'll be wonderful, the three of us together here."

They both had a sense of relief. Like they now had a little control over what was going on in all their lives. Marla went into the kitchen and brought back two cups of the tea that Ed had made, and they relaxed.

*****

Ed and Marla arrived at the hospital at about five that evening and went directly to the nurse's station and then to the waiting room. Dr. Morgan came to see them on his way to Sarah's room.

As they walked down the hall, he told them he had looked at her chart, talked with Dr. Stearns, and was aware of all that Dr. Stearns found during surgery. He had preliminary results from the lab and would get more detailed information tomorrow.

The sound coming from Sarah's room was unmistakable. She was jabbering away with the attending nurse. Looking up, she saw them enter her room. "Hi, you two! How are y'all doing? Hi, Dr.

Morgan," she said, smiling. Marla and Ed could do nothing but look at each other and smile.

Dr. Morgan looked at the nurse and asked how the patient was doing.

"Well, as soon as the sedative had mostly worn off, I found out there's nothing wrong with her lungs, her vocal cords, or her attitude. The rest is in her chart. If you want to know anything about her life, just ask me, and I can tell you."

The nurse was grinning from ear to ear. She had a tough job in hard situations, and she didn't often meet patients like Sarah. *What a joy being on duty with one who makes me smile*, she thought.

"Oh, Sarah!" Marla said lovingly.

Looking at the doctor, the nurse said, "I've just hung the last bag that's on the orders. I'll be back later." The nurse looked at Sarah and said, "You're something else. You know that?" Then she left the room smiling.

"That's my Sarah," Marla said again with a smile on her face. She realized that it was the first time she had smiled today.

Dr. Morgan pulled a chair over beside Sarah's bed. Marla sat in the other chair, and Ed stood beside her with his hand on her shoulder.

"Sarah," Dr. Morgan began, "first off, I have written orders for pain medication. Don't wait until you're in severe pain to tell the nurse you need something. They have a schedule for administering what I think will be enough, but they have orders for additional medication if you feel you need it. We'll do whatever we need for the next two days or so to see that your discomfort is minimal. Be sure to talk to the nurse on duty about how you feel always. okay?"

"Yes, Doctor. But whatever is in that bag up there coming into me is pretty good stuff. I never felt better in my life!" Sarah said. Everyone laughed.

"Well, Sarah," Dr. Morgan continued, "that's just a combination of the sedation from the surgery still in you and the pain meds you're being given. This feeling won't last through the night. You remember what I said, and you tell the night nurse if you need anything. Now let's discuss the surgery."

Sarah interrupted Dr. Morgan, "Doctor, I knew the results would either be really good or really bad. God and I've been discussing this for the last couple of days. I'm in his hands, and it's for his purpose. So don't try to gloss over the results or try to create some illusion. What do we have to do next? That's all I want to know."

Marla was astounded. Then she thought, *No, that's Sarah through and through. Sarah, you never stop teaching me or anyone else who comes into your life, do you?* Marla loved and admired her friend for just this reason.

"Thank you, Sarah," Dr. Morgan continued. "It's refreshing to talk to someone this plainly. Okay, in plain English… The cancer was extensive. It was in all of your reproductive organs, and Dr. Stearns had to remove them all, along with other areas and tissues that had cancerous growth. The bone-marrow biopsy showed that cancer had spread to the bone marrow. All this together points clearly to the fact that the cancer is a very aggressive one and has spread throughout your body, and it could and will reappear anywhere…

"Sarah, we can't cure you. But we can do many things. We could treat the cancer aggressively with chemotherapy, but the drugs we would have to use to fight the cancer would be in large dosage and would take a toll on your body. After each treatment, you'd be in pain for a few days. We could treat that pain with medication but not eliminate it entirely.

"You'd have severe nausea, which we could treat with medication but not eliminate entirely. You'd lose all of your body hair. And this would happen weekly for four to six weeks. Then we would reevaluate and discuss further treatment. You'd probably not be as mobile or as able to carry on life as you have been up to now. And there would be no guarantee of a cure.

"A second option would be to do nothing and to put you in hospice care. They would see that you were pain free and had as good a quality of life as could be expected for, as you know…as long as God wanted.

"There's a third option, which is what I recommend. It's palliative chemotherapy. Palliative care is specialized medical care for people living with a serious illness. This type of care is focused on providing relief from the symptoms and stress of the illness. The goal is to improve the quality of life for both the patient and the family. Palliative care is based on the needs of the patient, not on the patient's prognosis. The chemotherapy we'd be using would be to prolong a useful and meaningful life for as long as possible.

"You'd need to recover from your surgery for the next four to seven days. Once we were sure you've recovered fully from the surgery, we'd start your chemo treatment. We'd want you to undergo two cycles of chemo. A typical cycle for you would probably be three weeks. Then we would do a PET scan. It would tell us if and where cancer is present in your body, and we would evaluate the effectiveness of the previous treatment. It would be chemo in a non-curative setting to optimize symptom control, to improve quality of life, and to some extent, to improve survival.

"Sarah, I don't believe in end-of-life chemotherapy, which doesn't improve longevity or symptom control. I do not believe in trying to postpone the inevitable by creating undo anguish and discomfort in the patient. I do not believe in placating the family by creating a sense of hope that will not materialize at the expense of their loved one. Do you understand what I've said, and do you have any questions?"

"No questions," Sarah said calmly with tears in her eyes. As strong as she was, she had to admit that this was so difficult. She knew the reality of what was happening to her. But she couldn't be emotional now. She had to be practical. "I think the third option is best. What do you think, Marla?"

Marla was stunned by the manner in which Sarah posed the question. The doctor had just discussed end-of-life treatment. Marla's mind was trying to process the hundreds of things that Dr. Morgan spoke of, and now she had to answer a question. Suddenly, her mind went blank. She couldn't think and sat staring at her friend with a glazed look in her eyes.

"Marla," Sarah said, "I just love you. You always make me wonder what is going on in that mind of yours. Dr. Morgan gave me three options, and I want to know what you think."

Marla snapped out of it. "Oh, Sarah, I love you so much," she said.

"I know," Sarah replied. "Now let's stay on subject, shall we?"

Marla felt embarrassed. "I'm sorry," she said. "Sarah, this has to be your decision. But whatever you decide, I know it'll be the best decision, and I'll be right beside you. Always." Marla smiled at Sarah. It was a serious, loving, caring smile. Sarah read all that was showing on Marla's face.

"Doctor, I know that option three is the best for me, but I want to discuss it with my family. We're all in this together, and we need to agree on what God wants for me. One of us will call you tomorrow," Sarah stated as calmly as she could.

"I agree," the doctor said. "I'll wait to hear from you."

The doctor then left the room. There was a stillness in the room as the reality of the situation settled in on the three of them.

20

E D AND MARLA drove home after spending some time with Sarah. Marla had said that she would be back every day. Sarah already knew that and told Marla to go ahead and let everyone know how she was and what was going to be coming up. She didn't want to withhold any information from her church family and friends.

Sarah and Ed found Emma sitting on the couch, anxiously waiting for them when they arrived back home. Marla told Emma all that Dr. Morgan had said and what Sarah wanted. Marla emphasized that Sarah had been calm and accepting of things. No surprise there. However, tears were welling up in Emma's eyes as she and Marla hugged each other. Ed told Marla that he needed to leave, but they agreed to keep in touch with each other. Ed kissed Marla and left.

"Emma," Marla said, taking a deep breath, "I don't know what to think. This is all happening so fast."

"I know, Dear. I feel the same way." Wiping her eyes with a handkerchief, Emma said, "But we can't just sit around moping and thinking. Sarah knows what's coming, and she is being her practical, 'God is in control' self. We feel the same.

"We'll both go see Sarah in the morning. Then we can tell her about your plan to move her into my house. We both need to get on the phone now and call the people we need who can start the moving. I can get everyone over here after you bring me home tomorrow, and we can get started. The room is going to need some attention since it hasn't been used for anything but storage for so long."

Marla sighed. "You're right, Grandma. The best thing for the two of us right now is to keep busy."

They both started calling. It didn't take long to get some of the church friends to agree to come over. Everyone they called promised to be there when Emma was ready. Marla and Emma had agreed that Emma could be home by one in the afternoon. After all the phone calls, Marla and Emma had a light dinner. Both decided that they just wanted to go to bed. Neither of them would be able to sleep much even though they were exhausted.

Marla and Emma arrived at the hospital around nine the next morning and went into Sarah's room. It was a replay of the previous afternoon. The nurse who had been there the day before had told the night nurse what to expect from her patient that evening. Sarah lived up to her billing, even during the night.

Each time the night nurse came in to check on Sarah or hang a new bag of meds, Sarah would be aroused out of what light sleep she was getting in the hospital, and the conversation would pick up again. The nurse left Sarah's room each time that night with a big grin on her face. The night nurse explained about this special case in room 307 then left the day nurse in charge.

As Marla and Emma walked in, Sarah was well into breaking in this new day nurse.

"Then I broke the lamp—Oh, hi, you two! Come over here. I was just telling Mary...what was I telling you, Mary?" Sarah asked, looking at the nurse.

"You two take over for a while," the nurse said, looking at Marla and Emma. "My ears are ringing. She's doing fine obviously. No problems from a medical standpoint. I'll be back later, and you can finish whichever story you want to, Sarah."

She turned to leave, looked at Marla, smiled, and shook her head. Marla knew that smile. It was the same smile everyone had after meeting Sarah for the first time. Marla and Emma both went to the bed and gave Sarah a hug.

"I hope you brought something to eat," Sarah suddenly said. "Whoever they have in the kitchen needs to take some lessons. I don't know what they served for dinner last night. I think it was some kind of cardboard. And they must've gotten a good deal on Jell-O. It turns up on every tray."

"Sarah, you just had major surgery. What'd you expect? Steak and hot sauce?" Marla asked, almost laughing.

"No, I guess not. You're right again, Marla."

"Please be serious for just a little bit. We want to know how you are, and then we have something to talk about. Really, how're you feeling?"

"I'm having a little pain. It comes and goes. I try not to think about it. They give me medicine, and that helps. I really don't want to eat too much anyway, and they bring me very little. They say that's to keep me from being nauseous. They give me medicine to help with that too. The doctor doesn't want me moving for a few days. Then there's the worst part…"

She hesitated, and Marla and Emma had a momentary feeling of concern.

"I have to just lay here! I can't do anything. This is going to bore me to tears. All I have to do is lie here and wait for someone to come in so I can talk to them."

"Sarah, I don't know why I was concerned about your condition. It has not changed. Your condition is still Sarah." Marla smiled. "Emma, you tell her about the plans we have for when she comes home."

Emma proceeded to do that. "Sarah, we know you'll need help for a while, and we don't want you alone in your house. So Marla had a *practical* solution."

At Emma's emphasis on the word *practical*, the three of the them all grinned at the same time.

Emma continued, "You know, my back bedroom has been used to store things? Well, we already have a crew lined up to start this afternoon. We're going to move everything from the bedroom in your house to my house and set it up in my back bedroom. Your bedroom in your house will become my storage room. Your new room at my house will need some work, but we have more than enough people to get this done.

"Oh, Sarah, it'll be so nice. The three of us under one roof! We should have done this long ago. I guess you and I had just gotten so used to our lives as they were and never considered it."

Sarah looked at Marla with tears in her eyes. "Well, that's the most wonderful idea. I've always been independent and never asked for help. I always wanted to be able to take care of myself. But being practical, I know I'll need some help. Oh, you two, I am so blessed!"

Marla grabbed a tissue and wiped the tears from her friend's face. Then the three of them spent the rest of the morning talking. It was just another day in Sarah's life. That's the way Sarah had always lived.

21

M ARLA AND EMMA arrived home at about twelve thirty. They'd told the church friends to come at one. The women were both feeling better than they'd felt in days. It was like they didn't have to hold up the world. Like God had said, "I got this." They felt a sense of relief after talking with Sarah. But how could one not? She was filled with the joy of the Spirit.

When it was time to get to work, Marla looked at Emma. "I'm going to the office. I texted Ed, and he needs some help. If Sarah were here, she would scold me severely if I didn't do just that."

"I know, Dear, and that is exactly what you should do," Emma said. "I have this end under control. I just have to sit here and say, 'You do this, and you do that.' We'll have a good time for the next few days fixing the room up for Sarah. You don't think about this. Twenty other people and I have this. You take care of Sarah and Ed and in whatever order is needed for the next few days. We'll catch up on each other in the evenings, and you can tell me what's going on with Sarah. But you know, I've already heard most all the stories."

So it was like that for the next few days. Marla saw Sarah at the hospital first thing in the morning then drove to the office. She drove back each afternoon to see Sarah and then back to the office again. Marla was only at the office for a short time for each visit, but it was enough to get done whatever Ed needed done. He had no problem with it. He loved Marla, and he loved that she would make a couple of hours in each day to help him. It didn't go unnoticed. They also had lunch together each day. And Ed's fondness for her only continued to grow.

The two friends had such a joyful time when they were together in the hospital. It was different from being together on a couch, in a car, on a picnic, or down the aisles at Walmart. Even under difficult circumstances, they were growing closer. It was as if things had been planned that way.

Meanwhile, Emma was overseeing the renovation. She'd never been in control of so many people, and it was challenging. Everyone wanted to help, and help they did. Emma told everyone what the plan was when they first arrived. Then each got the picture and took off to do his or her part. The first chore was to get all the stuff out of Emma's spare bedroom. They took it all over to Sarah's house and put it in the living room until they had emptied her bedroom. Once they had Emma's spare bedroom cleared, a few of the men began sizing up the situation.

The ladies didn't have a problem with it and went in to be with Emma. Some tea, rest, and conversation sounded good to them. Meanwhile, Fred had left his hardware store for the afternoon to help with the work. He spoke up first since he knew more about what needed to be done than anyone else there.

"Well, this room needs some work," he said. "The carpet's a mess. I think we should get it cleaned. It's not stained but just looks dirty. I think that'll take care of it. We need to repaint the room, obviously. The bifold doors on the closet need new hardware. No problem. A new light fixture to replace the Depression-era piece and new curtains. I know the girls will buy those or sew some, and I think it'll be ready. I'm going to the store to get spackling and paint supplies, and we'll get started on repainting. You guys start getting ready for painting. I'll be back in a few minutes."

Fred explained to the ladies in Emma's living room what the plan was. Afterward, he left, and the chattering commenced.

"Oh, I've just the curtains for the windows!" one said.

"Or I can make some," another said.

"I have a great painting for a wall," said another.

And on and on it went. They all loved Sarah so and wanted the room to be just right when she saw it.

Marla was surprised each evening at the change that was taking place in her grandmother's house. It was apparent that much work was being done daily, and she thought she could still hear the happy voices that had been speaking there during the day as she walked through the house.

When she came home on the fourth evening, Marla found her grandmother sitting on the couch, knitting.

Emma looked up from her work and smiled, saying, "It's all finished. Come. Let's look at it together."

"Yes, let's," Marla said.

They walked into Sarah's new bedroom together. Marla thought it looked like a picture from a home-improvement magazine. They were met with freshly painted walls, ceiling, and trim. The carpet looked new. The curtains were perfect, bright, and colorful. A beautiful light fixture lit up the whole room. Someone had polished all of Sarah's furniture so carefully that it looked fresh from the furniture store. The windows were so clean that it seemed like there was no glass in them.

Sarah was a minimalist when it came to decorating. It was obvious that her friends thought some added touches would be nice. New books were stacked neatly in the bookcase, along with other items from Sarah's house. Pictures and paintings were hung appropriately on the walls. The nightstand by the bed and Sarah's dresser had been adorned with items from the homes of the churchwomen who had helped. Sarah had been a part of everyone's lives, and they honored her with those special touches. Fresh flowers were in a vase on the top of the bookcase and on the nightstand by the bed.

Marla started to cry. "Oh, Emma, it's just perfect! Sarah's going to love it."

"I know." Emma smiled. "The men decided to repaint the bathroom too, and they put handicap bars everywhere to aid Sarah. And I know I'll use them too. How is Sarah today?"

"Just as spunky as ever. She said the doctors told her if she keeps improving as she is, she can come home in two days, provided she remains in bed and rests. She said she wants to come home so badly she would even stop talking if that's all it took. I told her that wouldn't be necessary. 'Keep improving' doesn't mean you have to do something as spectacular as parting the Red Sea.

"The nurse told me that all the nurses who work that section hadn't had such an experience with a patient in a very long time. And she wasn't just referring to Sarah's personality. She also meant Sarah's faith. She said being around Sarah made them all reflect on their faith like they hadn't done before. She said one of the nurses had previously scheduled a few days off that week, but she canceled it so she could be on duty with Sarah at least once more. They all thought she was such a blessing, and they were all glad that Sarah had been a part of their lives, even if briefly."

On the sixth day, Marla was in the room with her friend. They were waiting quietly for Dr. Morgan to stop by on his afternoon rounds. However, another doctor entered the room.

"Hello, Sarah. I'm Dr. Fleming. Dr. Morgan was extremely busy in his office this afternoon and asked me to make his rounds for him. This isn't unusual. All the doctors on staff cover for one another.

"I've looked at your chart. Dr. Morgan said if I found no complications, I could sign the orders for you to be released. Are you feeling okay? The last thing any of us wants is for you to go home too early, have problems, and have to come right back."

"No, I really feel okay. My best friend and her grandmother are going to be taking care of me. I promise I'll do what I need to. I don't want to come back. You know the food here is really not very good," Sarah said with a grin on her face.

Dr. Fleming laughed. "Yes, I've heard some of the stories about you, Sarah. We all like to see our patients go home. But the nurse told me you will be missed. I want you to spend the night here just to err on the side of caution. I'm going to get with the charge nurse and get all the paperwork finished. I'll sign the order for you to be released early tomorrow, and I'll have a doctor on staff see you first thing in the morning just to be sure you're okay.

Dr. Fleming then turned to look at Marla. "I assume you are Marla?"

"Yes, I am," she replied.

"Come back here around eight tomorrow morning, and you can get her things together and take her home." Then Dr. Fleming turned to the patient for a final word. "Goodbye, Sarah."

"Goodbye, Doctor, and thank you," Sarah replied. "And by the way, I love your tie. Did you pick it out?"

The doctor smiled and said, "No, my wife did."

"Well, she has good taste."

"I know." The doctor grinned. "She married me."

"Oh, you're good! I wish you had time to talk," Sarah said, grinning back at him.

"Sorry. I'm on duty. Good evening, you two," the doctor said before he left the room.

Marla sat in her chair looking at Sarah, shaking her head, and smiling. Sarah glanced over at Marla.

"What're you looking at?" Sarah asked, smiling back.

22

MARLA AND EMMA arrived at the nurse's station promptly at eight the next morning. The nurse saw them approach and said, "You two go on in. She's been discharged. I was going in to help her change. Give me a minute to finish some paperwork, and I'll be in there to discuss everything with you."

Upon entering Sarah's room, they heard a cheery greeting. "Hi, you two! Hope I didn't get you up too early. I was sleeping pretty well when the nurse came in a while back and told me to wake up. This place is something else. They tell you to get some rest and then wake you up all the time to take more blood out of you or give you a pill to help you sleep. Hello? Just leave me alone, and I'll sleep just fine.

"Marla, I hope you have a sausage biscuit in your purse. I'm starving. I mean, how much Jell-O do they think a person can eat? I feel skinny as a rail. I must've lost twenty pounds in here, and I didn't have twenty pounds to lose. I can't wait to get back to Waterloo and my chair in your living room, Emma. I can't wait for a cup of tea from you, Marla. Has anyone been over to see you, Emma? You've probably been so lonely with me gone and Marla here with me and working—Well, cat got your tongue? Can't either of you say anything?"

Marla and Emma looked at each other with knowing expressions and walked to the bed, still not saying a word. Each leaned over and kissed Sarah on the cheek.

"I've been stuck in this place for a week, and all I get is a kiss? I appreciate it, but can't either of you say anything?"

"Sarah," Marla said very slowly and distinctly, "nothing has changed. We still can't get a word in edgewise!"

The nurse came in. "Okay, I have some things to go over with all of you. The doctor has sent the prescriptions for Sarah's medications to the pharmacy downstairs. They are for pain as needed, nausea as needed, and antibiotics on a daily basis for a while. Plus, some germicidal lotions for her abdomen. I've given Sarah written instructions for bathing and hygiene and other information for the next week. Please follow the instructions. They're for her health and protection. Dr. Morgan said he would contact you next week about starting chemo. Do you have any questions?"

Silence was their answer.

"Well, I guess that means you want to get out of here, Sarah. I can't blame you. Marla, get her clothes to wear home, and I'll help you change her," the nurse instructed.

After they had Sarah ready to leave, the nurse said for Marla to pack her things. Someone would come up to get Sarah, and Marla and Emma could get the car.

Marla said, "Emma and I will stop by the pharmacy, and we'll be waiting for you out front."

She and Emma left to do just that. Then they pulled the car over to the patient pickup area and waited and waited.

"Okay, it's taking them a long time to bring her down. What's going on?" Emma asked. Then she remembered. This was *Sarah* that the nurse was bringing down. And Sarah would have to recall some event in her past to share with others lest her life be deprived of such a moment. Far be it from Sarah to let that happen.

When the nurse was finally able to tear Sarah away from all those people she encountered on the way down the hall, she was relieved.

"I'm sorry it took me so long. We had to stop and talk to people all along the way," she said.

Marla looked at her and smiled as she helped Sarah into the front seat and said, "We know. Trust me. We *know*. Thank you."

All three were filled with excitement on the drive home. The cup of God's love for each of them was overflowing.

When they arrived at the house, Marla helped Sarah into her wheelchair. "Your things can wait. I want to get you inside. We have a surprise for you."

"I know," Sarah said matter-of-factly. "You told me you were going to have my bedroom furniture moved over here."

Marla grinned the kind of grin when you know you have a wonderful surprise for someone you care about.

"Well…" Marla teased, "a few people came over and did a few things, and, well, kind of did some touch-ups. Oh, Sarah, please be quiet just this once. Emma and I have been waiting for this moment for days!"

Sarah could tell by the tone of Marla's voice that her friend was serious. And whatever it was that Marla had planned, Sarah didn't want to spoil it. So she was going to do exactly what Marla wanted. For once, Sarah was going to be quiet.

Marla pushed her friend through the house and toward her new room. She pushed Sarah through the doorway and stopped so that Sarah could sit there for a moment and look at the room. Emma was close behind. The three of them remained quiet. When Marla leaned over to look at Sarah, she saw her friend's lips quivering and tears streaming down her cheeks as she examined the room from her wheelchair.

Marla was a little concerned. "Are you all right?"

"N-no," Sarah stammered. "I'm a hundred times better than all right. I can't believe what I see! I don't know what to say. Honest, I can't find the words. It looks like a picture in one of those beautiful home magazines. How did you two do this?"

"Well, actually, we did very little," Emma said. "Once the word got out to the church congregation, I had to schedule all the help. Everyone wanted to be over here at the same time. I made sure that everyone did a part of the work or furnished something. Sarah, every single friend from the church helped in this. It was a joint effort. Everyone loves you, Sarah, and I couldn't keep anyone away."

"Would someone please get me some tissues? I'm getting my shirt wet," Sarah said firmly. "And let go of my chair. I want to get in here and look at all this."

Emma left to find a box of tissues. Sarah realized that they had thought of everything. She went around the room, touching and looking at it all. Her friends had brought in so much more than just what Sarah had in her old room. There were knickknacks, pictures, flowers, a bookcase, new curtains, new paint, and lighting fixture! She knew that each item had a special meaning to the person who brought it.

"Marla, I've never felt so loved in all my life!" Sarah said.

Marla could feel the emotion in Sarah's voice. "You are loved by so many, Sarah."

Emma returned with the box of tissues and gave it to Sarah.

"You two go fix some tea," Sarah said to Marla and Emma. "I'll be in there shortly. I just want to sit here by myself for a while."

"Okay, Dear," Emma said as she left. Marla didn't say anything as she left.

After a while, Sarah finally got to the living room.

"Well," she said, "you two finally found a way to get me to stop talking! I still can't find the words to say what I feel in my heart. It'll take a day or two for this to sink in. But I need to find a way to thank all the ladies and men who made this happen. I'll write a letter of thanks and have Mary Gibbons insert it in the church bulletin Sunday. And now the three of us are living together! This is just too wonderful... I would like a cup of tea, though."

"Coming right up," Marla said, a twinkle in her eyes.

They sat in the living room and engaged in happy chatter. They were all so glad that Sarah was back home. A good day had just gotten a whole lot better.

23

THE NEXT FIVE days, Marla, Sarah, Emma, and Ed all settled into a routine; and they felt relieved to be able to do that. It returned a sense of normalcy to their lives. They were all aware of what was ahead in the coming weeks and months. But for now, they were enjoying each day.

A pattern developed: Marla would go into the office every other day and work a few hours. Then she and Ed would have lunch. She would next drive home for a short visit with Sarah then head back to the office.

Marla had learned the tasks that Ed wanted her to do. She took care of the paperwork, returned most of the calls on the answering machine, and fielded calls that came in while she was at the office. Ed was really enjoying his work now. He could do what he needed to do to grow his insurance agency: sell insurance. Meanwhile, Marla was taking care of the rest. They made a good team. Just as he had expected.

Emma had a new job too. She was in charge of scheduling visits for Sarah. When word got out that Sarah was home, Emma's phone never stopped ringing. Everyone wanted to visit their friend. Emma would have groups of two or three come at one time since her house was not suited for a large crowd, and she wanted the visits to be personal for the visitors and for Sarah. Emma became quite good at her job too. All morning, people would be coming and going until eleven thirty. She scheduled no visitors during lunchtime as Sarah needed to rest. Visiting hours resumed at two and ended at five.

Sarah was doing what the doctor had ordered; she was resting. The only part of her body that was moving was her mouth, and she couldn't have been happier. Sarah and her visitors chattered away, and a grand time was had by all. The evenings were reserved for just the new trio, as they called themselves. Ed often stopped by on his way home as well.

The days when Marla didn't go to work, she did the housekeeping and ran errands. She enjoyed having those times alone to think.

Dr. Morgan's office called during the week and scheduled Sarah to start her chemo treatment Tuesday morning of the following week. He had an appointment for her at ten on Monday for a consultation. They'd prepared themselves for this, knowing that the day was coming.

Sunday morning at the church was special. For the first time in her church life, Sarah could not corner anyone. Instead, she was constantly surrounded by a host of loving friends and couldn't have moved if she'd wanted to. Everyone was glad to see her in church. Her many friends talked about how much fun they had, had getting Sarah's room ready.

Pastor Baker had also prepared a special sermon. He said it was about a special kind of people—people like Sarah—and what great leaders they are because of how they lead by example. "This is what we have all learned about Sarah in the many years we have known her," he told the congregation.

The church bulletin listed Gal. 6:9–10 as the scripture passage for his sermon:

> Let us not grow tired of doing good, for in due
> time we shall reap our harvest, if we don't give up.
> So then, while we have the opportunity, let us do
> good for all, but especially to those who belong
> to the family of faith.

Pastor Baker was in rare form as he spoke. This was a message he knew was the heart and soul of his entire flock, not just Sarah. He loved to expound on witnessing the Word of God at work.

As he spoke, Marla sat in the pew, motionless. It was as if she were the only one in the congregation and Pastor Baker was speaking to her. She had always learned and understood the Sunday sermon.

But today was different. The events of the previous weeks had made a mark on her. She had felt so strongly that she was in God's will. The depth of the relationships with the ones she loved had grown, and the message she was listening to went deep into her heart.

Marla had known since the first day she had met Sarah that this girl was different—and special. She had learned a lot about Sarah, and she had learned to love her new friend. Now she had a glimpse into Sarah's soul with words she was hearing from the pulpit. Sarah was not only special; but she had also been a gift from God to all who knew her long before Marla had entered her life.

Marla thought, *I was just another soul God had allowed to cross Sarah's path.* Marla was not better, greater, or more deserving of the love that Sarah had to give than anyone else. Yes, they had a special relationship, and Marla felt that God had a plan for her to help take care of Sarah in the time to come. Many other women in the church could have done this for her, but Marla felt that God wanted it this way. And she knew Sarah felt the same.

Pastor Baker finished his sermon. Everyone in the congregation was opening a hymnal, and the pianist was playing the prelude to "Great Is Thy Faithfulness." Everyone was standing, except Sarah and Marla. Sarah poked Marla in the arm. Marla shook her head and, a little confused, looked at Sarah.

"It's not good to fall asleep during the sermon. What'll the neighbors think?" Sarah said with a smile on her face. She knew that was not the case. She could tell by the look on Marla's face.

"God just spoke to me during the sermon," Marla said with a look of pure joy on her face.

"I know, Dear. He spoke to all of us. But sometimes he speaks louder to some than others," Sarah replied. "Now stand up and sing with the rest of them. And sing it like you feel it."

Marla couldn't do anything but smile, shake her head, and join in the praise of song. She was in good voice today. "Great is thy faithfulness, oh, God our Father…"

24

THE GIRLS ARRIVED on Monday morning for the consultation with Dr. Morgan. They had no idea what was to come, but they knew no fear of the unknown as they had in the past few weeks. They both knew that there would be challenges for Sarah, but she and Marla had each other. No one was going to face anything alone. That gave the friends great comfort. The challenges of life could be met because each had God and her best friend at her side. Marla wheeled Sarah into the waiting room, both with the confidence that one feels when at peace.

"Sarah is here," Marla told the receptionist.

"Have a seat, and the nurse will be with you shortly. Please fill out these forms, and give them to the nurse when she calls you," the receptionist said as she handed out a clipboard with papers on it and closed the glass window.

Marla sat down in the chair beside Sarah. "I'll fill this out. It's just the same routine stuff."

"Okay," Sarah said, then turned to the person sitting beside her. "My name is Sarah. I love your dress."

And the conversations have begun, thought Marla as she started filling out the paperwork. Soon the nurse opened the door and called Sarah's name. Marla broke Sarah off midsentence. "We have to go," she said as she stood behind the wheelchair and started pushing her friend toward the door.

"Sorry, Mildred. I won't be able to finish my story. Miss Bossy here says I have to go. I hope everything works out okay for your daughter. Have a good day!"

"You too, Sarah," Mildred replied.

Sarah looked up at Marla, grinning from ear to ear.

"Oh, wipe that grin off your smug face!" Marla said, faking a grimace.

The nurse led them into an exam room and took Sarah's vitals. She then opened her file on the computer and filled in some information from the forms that Marla had filled out. "The doctor will be in shortly," she said as she left the room. The girls sat quietly and waited.

Dr. Morgan came right in and addressed each of them, "Good morning, Sarah, Marla."

"Good morning, Doctor," they both replied.

"Sarah, I want us to have a conversation about the treatment we are going to start you on. First thing you need to be aware of is how we will administer the drugs. In most cases where the cancer is advanced, we have a VAD surgically implanted in a large vein near the heart. In your case, we are not treating the cancer as aggressively as we might otherwise, as I have explained previously. We'll be giving you smaller doses intravenously. We'll also be giving you drugs by mouth. You'll be getting all that I feel is necessary and staying within the protocols of why we're treating you in this manner.

"You need to plan on being here for treatment a minimum of four hours per session. You'll be in a comfortable chair, and Marla can stay with you during the entire treatment. You can eat and drink, but you won't be mobile since you'll have an IV in your arm the entire time. Do you have any questions about this so far?"

"No," Sarah replied.

"Now, I want to tell you about the side effects. Chemotherapy is effective in treating cancer because it attacks and kills fast-growing cells. Since this is the natural characteristic of cancer cells—they are fast-growing cells—the chemo is going to destroy the cancer cells. Other fast-growing cells in your body are the hair follicles, the cells lining the stomach wall, and the bone marrow. And they will be destroyed too. We can't do anything about the hair loss, but it'll always grow back when the treatment is stopped.

"The nausea you will experience is because the lining of the stomach is affected, and the natural acid in the stomach now irritates the stomach lining. We can treat this effectively with anti-nausea medicine. The problem with the bone marrow is that your red and white blood cell production is diminished. This makes you vulnerable to infection and other problems. We'll be giving you medicine to boost your immune system and the production of red blood cells. Your muscles will feel tired and will ache at times. Your age will help and your good health, although not being able to walk means you're weaker than someone who is ambulatory…

"Sarah, I'm not telling you this to alarm you. As your doctor, I want you to know all the facts. I anticipate you'll have no problems and few side effects. And we can treat them effectively. Do you understand this?"

"Yes," Sarah answered.

"After the first treatment and the next day, you'll have a clearer picture of what to expect. Please don't be alarmed or afraid. We do this for many patients each week. Cancer doesn't discriminate. We treat children under the age of five, people in their nineties, and all ages in between. You'll be just fine.

"Finally, we need to talk about what every patient has on his mind… How long? You told me in the hospital not to create any illusions about your prognosis, so I'll give you the facts. Three out of four women live for at least one year with stage IV cancer that has metastasized to other parts of the body. For quite some time, you'll have as normal a life as you have always had.

"The day of the chemo will tire you, and you'll feel the effects the next day. The rest of the time, you should have no problems and should be able to carry on with your normal routine. I'll give you some information to read when you get home.

"If you have any questions during the treatment, don't hesitate to ask me or any of the nurses who will be administering to you. There'll always be a doctor who'll make rounds during the day for all patients receiving treatment. I've sent the prescriptions down to the pharmacy for all the meds I've been discussing. You can pick them up on your way out. Follow the instructions as they're listed."

"Thank you, Doctor," Sarah said. "I'll just take it one day at a time. That's what I do every day anyway." Turning to Marla, she said, "Do you want to say anything?"

"No. If you're okay, I'm okay. You're the one being treated. I'm just here to support you," Marla replied, looking a Sarah with love in her eyes.

"Thank you, Dr. Morgan. We'll be here tomorrow. We're now going someplace nice for lunch. Marla is buying."

"You didn't say anything about my taking you to lunch," Marla said, wrinkling her forehead.

"Just did," Sarah replied, grinning.

25

THE NEXT DAY, they arrived at the treatment wing of the clinic, went to the waiting room, filled out the paperwork, and waited. Shortly a nurse came and called for Sarah. They went to an area with six large sitting areas divided by flat surfaces, each with its own equipment. The nurse introduced herself, and so did Marla.

Nurse Susan asked Marla to help Sarah into one of the seats. She explained that prior to each treatment, they would draw multiple blood samples and take all the vital signs. She said that they could process one of the blood samples at this station and do a CBC test. It would tell them if there should be a problem that could cause them to postpone the treatment, and it would help them to develop a track record of how her body was recovering from the previous treatment.

The other blood samples would be sent to the lab for more detailed analyses, and the results would be sent to the oncologist. The rest were just to make sure that the patient was in good physical health and had no illness that would prevent treatment that day or expose other patients to an illness. After having Sarah's blood drawn, they could go back to the waiting room. One of the nurses in the chemo-administering room would be out to get them as soon as a chair was available.

Fifteen minutes later, a different nurse came into the waiting room and called for Sarah. Marla followed the nurse, pushing her friend. The room had at least a dozen chairs with equipment alongside each chair in the large room. They went to the only vacant chair.

"I'm Sylvia," the nurse said. "I'll be administering your therapy today. And you are?" she said, looking at Marla.

"I'm Marla, her best friend, and I'll be here with her for all her treatments."

"Good, Marla. It's always a comfort to have someone with a patient during treatment. You can help her into the chair."

The day continued as Dr. Morgan said it would. Sylvia inserted an IV and started a bag of saline drip. During the next five hours, the nurse hung different bags of meds and gave Sarah multiple injections and multiple pills. She said some of the injections and pills were chemo drugs; others were to prevent any reaction to the drugs she was getting.

It was pretty uneventful other than the fact that Sarah must have felt like a pincushion. Marla sat and watched. She was free to come and go from the room and left a few times because she wasn't worried about Sarah. The chemo was a new experience for Sarah. Sarah was a new experience for Sylvia.

Sylvia was tending to multiple patients, so she got a break occasionally. When she came back, Sarah picked up the story where she had left off. Sylvia didn't mind. She learned quickly that Sarah had a good heart and was honest and sincere. She just loved to talk. Sylvia knew all too well that a lot of the patients treated here were, understandably, not of such good spirits. But to witness such joy in such adversity was refreshing. Sarah had left her mark in this place.

After the treatment was finished, Sylvia took her patient's vital signs. The girls were told to wait for fifteen minutes to be sure there were no side effects before Sarah left. Sylvia gave them instructions to follow and reminded Sarah to drink lots of fluids during the rest of the day. This was to prevent dehydration and help her kidneys flush out the chemo drugs.

As Marla pushed Sarah out of the room, Sarah said goodbye to each of the nurses. As well, they each told her goodbye. Then Marla drove the car to the patient pickup area. They had been using one of the wheelchairs provided by the clinic. She got Sarah into the car and returned the wheelchair to the entrance of the clinic. Soon after, they left to drive home.

"Sarah, those nurses have other patients they have to tend to. I don't think you should stop them from helping the other people there."

"Oh, Marla, always so serious!" Sarah said. "I would never do that. I know what they're doing. I was just making a little polite conversation."

"Sarah, you've never carried on just a little conversation!" Marla joked.

"Well, just for that, I'm not going to say a word to you on the way home, so there," Sarah said, looking at Marla with a smirk on her face.

Marla thought, *We'll see how long this lasts.* After about three minutes, Marla said, "Are you feeling okay? No side effects from the treatment?"

That got Sarah started. She had already forgotten what she had said three minutes ago and proceeded to recall the events of the day in detail. Marla settled back in her seat to enjoy the ride home.

When they got home, they saw that Emma was in her usual place, working on some knitting. "Hi, you two," she said when they entered the room. "How did it go?"

"Oh, it was nothing. I just sat in a chair and watched. Sometimes I'd get up and go in the waiting room just to move around or get something to snack on. Most of the time, it was pretty boring," Marla stated matter-of-factly.

"She was asking *me*, you ninny," Sarah said, trying not to laugh. "I was the one they were sticking needles in, and it was my body they were turning into a toxic waste dump."

"Oh, yes," Marla said innocently. Laughing, she leaned over and gave Sarah a kiss on her cheek.

"She was a lot braver than I think I would have been," Marla relayed to Emma. "Sarah, get in your chair, and tell Emma the same story you told me on the way home. I'm going to get you a glass of ice water. No tea for today. Remember, no caffeine."

When she turned to go into the kitchen, Sarah had already started telling Emma about her day. Overall, the three spent a quiet afternoon together. Ed came over after work, as they had previously arranged; and the four of them had a nice dinner. There was plenty to choose from. The three women wondered if they would ever have to cook again. Each day, one of the church friends brought over another special dish. Ed was having the time of his life as he hadn't eaten this well in his adult life.

It was decided that they needed some help eating all the food that was constantly being replenished. After dinner, they sat in the living room and talked. It was obvious that Sarah was not quite like her usual self, but she said she was not in any pain. She just felt worn out just the way Dr. Morgan had described. When Sarah was ready to turn in for the evening, it was agreed that the others would do the same. Sarah and Emma went to their rooms, but Marla stayed with Ed for a little while. They really wanted to talk to each other. The conversation between them had grown more personal as they were learning more and more about each other.

Later at night, Marla got up a couple of times to check on her friend. The doctor had given Sarah something to help her sleep, and she was very tired. Each time Marla checked in on her, Sarah was asleep. They had bought a bell for Sarah's nightstand so she wouldn't need to get up in the middle of the night by herself. Once Sarah rang the bell, Marla came in a moment, helping Sarah to the bathroom and back to bed. With only a few words spoken, both were soon back to bed.

The next morning, Marla found Sarah awake and reading her Bible. Marla asked, "Have you been up long?"

"Only a few minutes. I've had enough sleep but didn't feel like jumping out of bed. So I'm just taking it easy."

"That sounds very practical, Sarah. I'm going to get you some juice before I leave for work. I'll be right back."

"Okay." Sarah smiled at Marla.

Marla found Emma sitting on the couch, and she told Emma about last night and this morning. Emma said she was fine, and many ladies were going to come and sit with her and be here to help with Sarah if they were needed.

Upon arriving back home after a couple of hours at the office, Marla found Emma and two other ladies conversing in the living room. "Is Sarah still in her room?" she asked.

"Yes," Emma replied. "She wanted to rest in bed."

Marla immediately went in to check on her friend. "Are you okay? Is anything wrong?" she asked.

"I feel pretty much like Dr. Morgan said I would feel. Like I did when I fell out of a tree when I was ten years old. Wouldn't want to know what it feels like if they give you the full-dose chemo treatments. I just need to rest. I'll feel better tomorrow."

She wasn't up to spending time with some ladies from the church who had come by.

"This is your call, Sarah. You don't have to please others when you feel rough. This is why we prepared this private sanctuary for you. Emma will entertain the visitors you don't feel like seeing."

26

LATER THAT AFTERNOON, before Marla left for the office, Sarah said that she wanted to sit in the living room with Emma to greet her guests. She was feeling much better and really wanted to get out of bed. Marla had helped her bathe and get dressed.

The two of them were in good spirits now. It was a start to a new way of life for all. They knew they would be able to handle it, and now they couldn't wait for tomorrow. When Marla left to go to the office, Sarah was her old self, filling the hearts of those souls in her presence. That's what Sarah did best, and she was in her best form today. She'd faced the worst, and the worst had met its match.

On Thursday morning, Sarah rang her bell at six thirty in the morning. Luckily for Marla, she was already awake and had been up for a few minutes. Marla walked into Sarah's room, rubbing her eyes like she'd just woken up. "Can't a body get any sleep around here?" She moaned.

"Room service! Where's my breakfast? I've things to do and people to see. Don't have time to dilly-dally."

They both laughed out loud. Laughing's a good way to start any day.

"My, you're in fine spirits today! I'm glad to see it."

"Yes, as a matter of fact, I am. I want out of this room. I really feel like my old self today. That ol' Doc Morgan told it right. Take me to see Emma. I'll have my tablespoon of breakfast on the east-wing patio this morning," Sarah said with an English accent.

"Yes, my lady. As you wish," Marla said, mimicking Sarah.

She told Sarah about her new work schedule at the office with Ed. Marla explained that it would still leave plenty of time for the two friends and for Sarah to get back into her life's work.

Mrs. Rodriguez would come over and clean Emma's house on Monday, as she used to do at Sarah's. The woman now needed to work more hours and would get her pay doubled. She would also get a bonus of a casserole or two each week. That part would be their secret. Mrs. Rodriguez could hardly hold back her emotions when they told her all of this. She left praising God.

Sarah and Sue Jones would try and continue the trips to Laurens to the assisted-living homes as they always had when Sarah felt up to it. They didn't want their friend, Mrs. Reynolds, to be hurt because they didn't show up.

Tuesday was chemo day. The Tuesday Rummy games would be rescheduled to Saturday since that was the day Emma and Sarah spent together anyway.

Wednesday's volunteer time at the library in Laurens would be covered by Marla. It was best that nothing was planned for Sarah for that morning.

Thursday would remain the same with Millie, Sarah, and Emma at the market. "Don't want to leave out that Millie. She is such a talker," Marla reminded Sarah. They laughed at that. Marla said she might join them one morning. She said that she wanted to be in on the apple-picking conversation. Sarah mentioned that she had a pillowcase to finish for the pastor even though his birthday had passed. To her, a belated gift was better than none, and the pastor would understand.

On Friday, Bill Perkins was to come over. There was a spirited debate about whether Sarah should continue to discuss with him the many topics that she thought she should share with him while he did his work, or just leave him to his yardwork alone. They tabled that discussion for another time.

Saturday and Sunday remained pretty much the same. Of course, Sunday would never change—that was the Lord's day. Thus, the next weeks progressed.

Nothing had really changed in Sarah's life, except for her having to go to chemo on Tuesday and recovering on Wednesday morning. She had lost a few hours, but it was nothing to her. She would make up for the lost hours with the hours she had. Nothing was going to stop Sarah from completing her rounds. She had work to do for the Lord, and she would find the time (and hopefully the energy) to do it.

Many people were coming and going at Emma's house each day. With two live-in granddaughters, it was always like Christmas, and Emma had never been happier. Her house was the center of attention in Waterloo. She didn't know if that old screen door could take it. But the old woman knew what that slamming sound meant.

She came from a time when a screen door was the standard fixture in a home. And when the sound of that screen door slammed against the doorjamb, it was the announcement that someone they knew or loved had come to visit. Emma remembered it clearly. "Welcome," it said to whomever entered. What happy memories it brought to mind!

She had experienced a good life as a child. Her parents lived through the Great Depression and the Second World War. They had told Emma stories about difficulties in those times. That's what produced strong character in the people of Emma's age. They had known hard times unlike today's young people.

Because she had outlived many of her relatives, or they had moved away out of her life, Sarah's moving in next door was a blessing for both of them. Emma had a family, if only one member. But now the family had grown beyond her wildest dreams. That screen door slamming, the comings and goings…they were music to her old ears.

When Sarah came into her life, Emma had discovered a good friend, and Sarah had brought more friends into Emma's life than she ever could have dreamed. These recent days, Marla being back made it even better. Better still, Marla had changed. The caterpillar had changed into a chrysalis, and a transformation was taking place. First, the clothing and then her spiritual life. Her purpose in life and her priorities had changed. Anything on the outside was not as important to her anymore. A new inner world had opened.

Her teachers were in control now. Both of them. One spoke to her mind every day; the other spoke to her heart. Her heart's teacher was Christ; and he had given her Sarah, a friend and companion.

And then there was Ed. Marla had dated other men. Many men had asked her out, and Marla had fielded so many requests that she couldn't count them. Most were dismissed with a polite "Sorry. I'm busy then." When an exceptional man approached her, she wouldn't turn him down. She'd been in a few relationships, but they never evolved into much. Marla was Marla and was not going to give her emotions over to a casual relationship with just any man. So they would come and go.

What she had discovered in those men didn't exist in Ed. Now and then, she wondered, *Have I changed?* Ed was special. He was a good man, and Marla knew from experience that there aren't that many good men in this world.

For these two people who'd been attracted to each other to meet in Waterloo, South Carolina, it wasn't a coincidence. With God, there are no coincidences. This was planned, and Marla was going to trust God for how their relationship would progress. For the first time in her life, Marla knew that she was in love. She felt it with Sarah. She felt it with Ed.

The following weeks moved as planned, and Sarah managed to continue her work for God yet still have time to rest when needed. Emma was enjoying each day now, and Marla could help the man she loved fulfill the dream of owning his own insurance agency. The time that Marla and Ed could be together at work and at home in the evenings was an important consideration, and Marla could have as much time as she needed and wanted to care for her friend. She wanted to be with Sarah as much as possible during this period of treatment.

And so it was. The days turned into weeks, and the weeks turned into many more weeks.

Sarah's treatments went well. Tuesdays were treatment days, and Sarah endured them. She could tolerate more discomfort than most people, and she had someone to lean on who took the burden away.

Wednesday mornings after treatments were times to rest. Then, by most Wednesday afternoons, she usually felt better and could get involved in the events of life—life at full throttle. The chemo was just a momentary distraction.

Emma was the quintessential grandmother. She had it all, and she didn't even have to cook. To really no one's surprise, the food cornucopia continued to overflow on Emma's table and in her refrigerator.

Ed had started attending a gym close by. With all that great food at Emma's, he knew he had to do something.

Marla recalled the day she had first pulled up into Emma's driveway so very long ago. She had thought, *I need a place to catch my breath, and then I'll move on.* It often occurred to her now how differently our plans sometimes turn out. As we look back on the events of our lives, we often can recognize God's hand at work.

Having undergone a metamorphosis, she had emerged as a beautiful, joyous creature of God. And it was plain to all who knew her that Marla had become a close companion to Sarah. Emma's two granddaughters were inseparable friends.

27

AS THE GIRLS settled in on the life that was now theirs, the last of the summer days' warmth had changed into the soft breezes of autumn. The smell of freshly cut grass occasionally lingered in the air as lawns still needed mowing. Songs coming from young girls skipping rope occasionally rang out: "Johnny gave me apples. Johnny gave me pears. Johnny gave me fifty cents to kiss him on the stairs…"

The breeze echoed the melody as it passed through the green canopy of the pines. The *cheer-cheer-cheer* song of the cardinals joined in on the chorus that filled the neighborhood. It was accompanied by the voices of two neighbors happily sharing the events of each other's day in one's front yard. God was in the process of changing his world.

Set on a county road, Emma's house was away from the noise of highway traffic. One had a sense of peace while sitting side by side on the swing on Emma's porch, far removed from the cares of the world. Both Sarah and Marla did this more often than not in the afternoons. It became a special time for them, and they were growing closer each day. They watched the changes in nature with the passing of time; with the setting of the sun.

God is subtle, but the beauty is in knowing that he is in control and will give the observer much to enjoy. Slowly, the leaves on the white ash, cherry, and river birch trees were starting to lose their green; and the colors of fall began slowly to come forth. The common nighthawk had already migrated. The migration of the broadwinged hawk had begun in the mountains; and if one looked closely, one could see a few tree swallows on their way to the coast.

The mornings began to have a crisp coolness to them; and the light of the day gave way, minute by minute, to the dark of night. The north wind created a ballet of leaves as they danced across the yards that were the stage. The ominous song of the north wind through the bare branches of the trees was a foretelling of the months to come.

After a few killing frosts came and went, the green of spring and summer had faded for another year. The green had left the ground but not the canopies of some trees. The needles of the pines and the leaves of the magnolia were a stark and welcome contrast to the bare branches of the deciduous trees. The flowers of the pansy and dianthus plants had replaced the marigolds and petunias in the beds in town. There was still beauty around for one to see. The last of the autumn days passed into the first days of winter without fanfare. Only the coolness of the afternoons separated the two seasons now.

Bill Perkins no longer came over since the grass was hibernating until spring, and he had long ago cleared the yard of fall debris. His mower had been left properly in its place in his garage, awaiting its chance to manicure the green grass of spring. His long afternoons with Sarah passed with the seasons. The time outdoors was still pleasant with the proper clothes and a good blanket on some days.

A couple of the men from church had built a firepit in Emma's backyard and laid pavers to it so that Sarah could go out there in her motorized scooter chair. Someone always came over and made sure that the women had plenty of firewood stacked. The trio could enjoy a nice fire on a cool, still afternoon; and they found those times especially enjoyable.

Marla sometimes took Sarah out to the lake for a quiet day. Sitting in silence, they could enjoy the beauty that God had created. The ducks performed their dance, webbed feet speaking their silent lines as they fanned the air. They pirouetted in the water, beaks down, in search of food. It seemed the fish wanted to be in the performance as they jumped to join in.

A few geese strolled through the scene as if the others were not there. Though arrogant, they were a beauty to behold. The previous performers continued as the gaggle moved on. A bald eagle swooped down, and rose with a trout in its claws for its evening meal. The chatter of a squirrel would occasionally break the silence.

The friendship the two felt for each other was profound. Words were not needed to add to the experience. They found many special ways to enjoy each other's company. A day in the park on a cool, crisp afternoon was a special treat for Sarah. It was for both. They had each said so.

The cold of winter settled in on Waterloo. The squirrels scurried through the yard, planting acorns for dinner or a young oak tree; only God knew which of the two they would become. The bird feeders needed constant filling as the invited guests enjoyed the bounty placed there for them. The occasional warm day was a welcome respite from the gray days. A walk outside on such a day was a gift cherished by those who partook of it.

Marla would wrap Sarah up in a blanket, and they would stroll down Emma's road. All the while, Marla pushed Sarah in her wheelchair. Fortunately, there was no traffic. They often engaged in trivial conversation. There was nothing they remembered after the journey, save for the joy of the journey itself.

Then the cold of January faded into the chill of February. The first robin appeared to those who watched. It may have been just a robin to many, but it was special to those with old memories. Those who recalled their grandmothers speaking of such things. The daffodils and tulips were showing off their splendor before the rest of nature. Boreas, god of North Wind, was soon to leave the scene. If one looked closely at the tips of the tree branches of the South Carolina peach trees, one might see the first buds of new growth.

No, winter had not left the scene, but spring was preparing for its entrance. Spring in all its splendor would adorn the earth as it had for all millennia. With the change in seasons came the spring rains, which were always followed by God's promise in the sky: a rainbow. A reminder that God keeps his word. To see such beauty is to feel joy in one's heart. The girlfriends tried never to miss a rainbow. And then the dark clouds would fade away, and the rains that fell would adorn the earth with new life again.

God's plan for his earth would be renewed and would continue.

28

THE AZALEAS WERE in full bloom now. The rose beds spoke of their special beauty and perfumed the air with their fragrance. And to that, they spoke very well. New growth adorned the canopies of the trees. The beauty of God's renewed creation was evident in all of nature.

Sarah and Marla were on the back porch overseeing their tiny part of that creation. They were sensitive to all of its beauty. Surely, God smiled at their understanding. The three of them—Sarah, Marla, and God—were one this morning. Blessed are they who see beautiful things in humble places, where others see nothing.

Marla sometimes reflected on her time at Waterloo. She looked back to the day she had first arrived at her grandmother's house. *Had that been a long time ago? Or only a few moments?* Since coming here for a short break to decide on her next path in life, she'd taken many steps. Really, she'd learned so much about how to live on the journey that God gives. Each person Marla had met had been a lesson for her, and her soul had been nourished.

Once seeking happiness, she had found it a hopeless, elusive search. Now she found what any soul is really searching for: joy. She had found joy, and the source of it never stopped its flowing. It was not linked to a fleeting experience but to something eternal. God was the fountain that sustained joy in the hearts of his people. The source ran deep, beyond understanding.

Yes, Marla thought, *you found love and joy when you were not even looking for them.* They'd been given to her by all the people in her life here. Not just Sarah, Ed, and Emma, but all the people of Waterloo who were her family now.

Sarah interrupted, "I'm feeling a chill from the breeze. Would you get me a blanket?"

"Of course," Marla replied and immediately stood up.

They looked at each other with a smile. Marla came back promptly with a blanket and placed it lovingly around her friend, making sure that Sarah was completely wrapped.

"Thank you," Sarah said.

"You're welcome," Marla replied, returning to her seat.

She thought, *The joy that God gives is a light he places in the hearts of his faithful. This light shines through those faithful souls, a beacon announcing God's presence in the dark places of his world. Mankind is drawn to light. God's light is seen by all, but some do not understand its source.*

Sarah had taught her friend about this light, and now it shone brightly in Marla. But just as some are drawn to light, others are drawn to the darkness of the world. Marla had once been drawn to this darkness. She was attracted to the superficial. But she'd been around Sarah's light for a while now. Sarah's light shone from the moment she awoke in the morning until she closed her eyes at night. Marla knew that this was one of the reasons she always wanted to be with her friend.

She also thought about the change in Sarah. It had appeared slowly. Other people in her life had always been foremost in Sarah's mind. But lately, Marla had noticed that a quietness had crept into Sarah's manner. Her friend was often reflective; and by the end of the day, she was tired and eager to go to bed.

Marla refused to think of why this was. Always attentive to her friend's needs, she didn't want Sarah to confirm her fears. So she hid them in the deep well of her mind, where people put realities they don't want to face. Each evening that they sat together with Emma on the porch or on the couch meant that they had been able to proceed on their journey together for another day. Marla woke each morning with the fear creeping out of its hiding place in her mind. *Would this be the day?* She would quickly push the thought back.

Another Monday came, and Sarah was preparing for their trip to Laurens and the assisted-living home for their weekly visit. Emma said that they have so many cookies and cakes that she would invite a few extra ladies over this afternoon to be here, when Sarah and Sue were to talk about the day they had spent. Marla said that she would plan on being around then too. They would make it a grand social event. The house would look immaculate since Mrs. Rodriguez said she would spend a little extra time making everything just so. Sarah seemed to be in pretty good spirits, and it pleased Marla to see this.

It was a typical Monday, and they were looking forward to the afternoon. Marla arrived back home shortly after two. Sarah and Sue had planned to be back around two thirty. Emma and Mrs. Rodriguez had everything ready for the guests. Emma had invited six ladies over. When Sarah and Sue came in, they exchanged greetings. Sarah said she wanted to go into her bedroom and lie down for a while until everyone arrived. Marla went with her.

"Are you okay?" Marla asked, a little concerned.

"I'm fine, really," Sarah said. "I'm just a little tired, and I want to be able to enjoy everyone coming over. I'll just lie in bed and close my eyes for a few minutes, and I'll be in as soon as I hear everyone. Go on and see if Emma needs anything. I'd tell you if something was wrong."

Marla looked at Sarah and smiled. "Okay," Marla said as she turned around and walked back into the living room.

Within about thirty minutes, all the guests had arrived, and the voices coming from the main room told Sarah as much. She got out of bed and joined them. Once there, she was the Sarah that everyone had always known and enjoyed being with.

29

T HE NEXT MORNING, Marla was helping her friend get ready for chemo. Sarah would be reclining in a large, comfortable chair, but it was still a tiring experience. Energy conserved in the morning was energy saved for later, Marla had explained. It made good, practical sense to Sarah.

At the clinic, the nurse had the CBC count. She came over to talk to Sarah.

"Your hemoglobin count's been dropping the last few weeks, and it's getting to the borderline. Dr. Morgan's making rounds today in the clinic. He can talk to you about it when he sees you. But there's nothing that would postpone your treatment today."

The nurse finished with her work, and then they were permitted to leave. Marla took her friend back into the waiting room.

Sarah spoke up. "I know your mind, Marla. Let it go. If it was really bad, the nurse would have said more about it. Dr. Morgan will explain. Remember, it's not your job to understand and find solutions."

Sarah looked directly into Marla's eyes with that look that Marla had seen countless times. It spoke volumes, and she understood. It meant "Chill out, Marla. We're in good hands." Marla knew. So she smiled back and nodded a few times. They waited for the chemo nurse to take them back for treatment. Once the nurse had started Sarah's treatment, they settled into the routine that they knew so well.

"Hi, Brenda! How is Bobby recovering from his broken arm?"

"Marcie, I love what you've done with your hair."

"Cindy, I can't wait to hear how Frank is doing with this new job."

And so it went until Dr. Morgan came onto the floor. He made his rounds and finally reached Sarah's chair.

"Hello, Sarah and Marla," he said. Looking at Sarah, he asked, "You feeling a little more tired lately?"

"Yes," she said. "Quite a bit."

"Have you been taking the vitamins and supplements I wanted you to have? And have you been eating the vegetables that help with the anemia?"

"Yes, we've been careful to watch my diet. We know what I should eat and try to get as much into my diet as possible."

"Well, this is not uncommon during long chemotherapy, so don't be concerned. We can only do so much with drugs and diet to prevent anemia. But if your red-blood-cell count was any lower, it would be a cause of concern because it would create a lot of other potential issues. We just need to give you a transfusion to get your count back up where it needs to be.

"We can schedule you to go after your treatment, but you must know that the transfusion itself will take four hours. And there'll be other checks that have to be done before the actual transfusion begins and after. You would probably be another six hours here today after your chemotherapy. So today would be a long day. You can come back tomorrow, if you want to. But I don't want you to put it off longer than tomorrow."

After the doctor explained, he waited for Sarah's response.

"Doctor, I really don't want to be here late tonight. I haven't had any real issues the mornings after my treatments. I'd rather come back in the morning," Sarah answered.

"Fine. I'll write the orders and give them to the charge nurse. She'll have everything scheduled by the time you leave. The receptionist will have all the information you need and will tell you where the IV will be administered. You can get all that from her when you leave, okay?"

"Yes."

"Now, let's discuss everything else."

The doctor and Sarah began their usual exchange about how she was doing and how her treatment was progressing. Marla just watched and listened. She knew her job, and it was a job she loved—being with Sarah in every step she took. That's what she told Sarah at the outset, and she knew deep down in her heart that this was what Sarah really wanted and needed. To know that Marla was with her. Marla was beside her. Marla was not going to leave her. Even Sarah, with all her strength and resources, would have trouble dealing with all this alone.

Sarah often said, "Thank you for being here with me, Marla."

After the treatment, the girls went home as usual. It was a typical Tuesday afternoon after the treatment. They settled themselves out on the back porch to take in the wonders of the day, as well as the creatures God had placed in their view for the enjoyment of the viewers. The beauty of nature in Emma's backyard was spectacular in the eyes of the two friends.

It had been another good day. Marla had finally learned this lesson from her teacher. Every day that God gives you is a good day. Serve him as best you can that day. Sarah could face anything because whatever the trial, whatever the challenge, it was a good day. Even Sarah was still learning, still being taught every day. The lessons never stop; life, after all, is a journey of lessons. Marla understood that now. She was starting to see and live and understand life as Sarah did.

They went in early the next morning for the transfusion. It was routine to those tending to Sarah, so the girls just tried their best to fit themselves into the routine. Even with the many preliminaries. Dr. Morgan had said that it would require a good deal of time for the blood to drip, insuring no reaction to the IV solution. All in all, it was uneventful. Just a long process.

The two companions arrived home late that afternoon, both tired. They were hungry and immediately went to the kitchen to look over the selection. Marla fixed Sarah a plate of her favorite choices and took it to her out on the back porch. Then Marla fixed a plate for herself and joined her friend. They enjoyed their meal, relaxing from the two previous days. Though tired, they felt the relief of knowing that a bad experience was over. They had faced it, survived it, and were glad to be home.

Ed came over later and joined them on the back porch. The three of them were together that evening; and Emma was on her couch, thinking about the many visitors of her day. All was right with their world.

30

THE REST OF the week passed by smoothly. Sarah thought that she felt better the two days after the transfusion than she had the two weeks prior. She seemed to be her old self again. But when Sunday came, she realized when she got up to get ready for church that the tiredness she had felt before the transfusion was back. She chalked it up to the busy week. She, Marla, and Emma went about their usual Sunday routine. Sarah pulled from her bottomless bucket of inner strength, and no one thought she was any different from any other Sunday.

But Sarah knew when they arrived back home from church that she wasn't the same. She wasn't going to spoil everyone's Sunday by bringing up a complaint that Marla would probably blow out of proportion. Determined to enjoy the rest of the day and the next, she wanted everyone else to do the same. With her inner resolve, which had always helped her to overcome whatever obstacle lay in the path, Sarah decided that this was another challenge God had placed before her. And she wasn't going to disappoint him.

When Tuesday morning came, she prepared and talked as if it were just another in the long string of what Tuesdays were now.

Once at the clinic and in the blood-draw phase of the treatment process, Sarah sat silently, eagerly awaiting what the nurse would say about her CBC. After the initial assessment that Sarah was normal, the nurse said, "Your hemoglobin is up from what it was last Tuesday, but it's still below where we would like it to be. And your white-blood-cell count isn't getting any better. Dr. Morgan will discuss this with you. It's okay. You're not in any immediate danger, and we can proceed with your treatment today. Marla, you can take her back into the waiting room."

Marla took Sarah to a corner of the waiting room where they could talk privately. Yet again, Sarah spoke directly to her friend.

"Marla, I love you. I don't think I could have come this far without you. I'll never be able to thank you enough for the support you've given me. The last nine or so months have been the best of my life. God said the number of our days was written in the Book of Life, before the creation was formed.

"I've always thought that it's not so much the number of our days that's important, but it's the quality of our days. Dr. Morgan told us that this time of treatment wouldn't last long. Remember? So we're not going to discuss anything here and now. We're going to go in there when they call us, get my treatment over with, and see what the doctor has to say. God's in control. Everything is according to his plan. Okay?"

"Okay," Marla replied with a faint smile and a tear.

There was no point in discussing her speculation; Sarah would have none of it. It was just another lesson from the teacher. No matter what the circumstances, good or bad, Marla was ever learning from Sarah. She had to choose between faith in God or faith in herself. And God had brought her here, to the end of her rope. It's where one finds oneself, at the end of a great trial. When all the resources, all the will that one has, all the love that can be poured out, can't stop the passage of time. It's then when a person has to let go.

Finally, there is a hollow feeling inside, like there's nothing under one's skin. Marla had been on this journey—a journey of heart and soul. But she wouldn't admit it to Sarah or Ed or anyone else. She didn't want to admit it to herself even though she lived with it every day. Marla knew she was totally empty of resources. If she didn't turn herself totally and completely over to God and accept whatever he chose to happen, she would be lost.

She took a deep breath, closed her eyes, and prayed. *I give up, God. I can't handle this alone any longer*, she thought. *I give it over to you. I know you have blessed Sarah. I know you have blessed me with the time you have given for Sarah to be with me.* She took another deep breath. The problem hadn't gone away, but the anxiety didn't seem to be as pronounced in her mind any longer. Still, she felt hollow inside.

The nurse came into the waiting room and walked over to them. She had been working here for a long time, and she knew what it meant when patients sat in that corner talking quietly. "It's time to take Sarah in," she said softly with a knowing sadness.

Marla looked up at the nurse, hesitating for a while, and then said, "Okay." They followed the nurse into the chemo room, and Marla got Sarah settled into her chair.

"I like your necklace," Sarah said, looking at the nurse. "Did you buy it, or was it a gift?"

"Actually," Bonnie said, "it was a gift from my husband many years ago. I saw it in my jewelry case this morning and realized I haven't worn it in quite some time."

"Well, it's quite lovely," Sarah said, smiling.

Marla slumped into her chair. She couldn't find words to say to anyone at the moment and hoped that no one would try to talk to her. She wanted to be alone. She knew Bonnie would be a little while getting the IV and the treatment started, and Sarah would want to do nothing more than what she was doing—bringing her joy into the lives of those around her with no thought of their conversation in the waiting room.

Marla said, "I'm going to the restroom and sit outside for a few minutes."

Sarah looked up at Marla and smiled knowingly. "I understand."

Marla went back into the waiting room and into the corner where she had been before. She didn't want to be around conversation.

Dr. Morgan made his way to Sarah after visiting with his other patients. Marla had come back in from the waiting room. He didn't ask Sarah how she was feeling. He knew.

He said, "Sarah, the transfusion did raise your hemoglobin but not significantly. I'll have the nurse let me know when your treatment is over."

"Okay, Doctor," Sarah said.

She looked at her friend. "Hold my hand."

Marla held her friend's hand firmly. They looked into each other's eyes and smiled. Sarah turned and looked straight ahead. They remained that way for the rest of the treatment. Sarah was quiet, responding with a smile to anyone who approached her.

31

WHEN SARAH'S TREATMENT was finished, they waited for Dr. Morgan. The doctor came in, walked over to them, and smiled. "Let's go to a room where we can talk," he said. They followed him into an exam room, and he pulled a chair over, in front of Sarah. Marla took her friend's hand in hers.

"Sarah, your CBC and other blood-work reports I get paint a pretty clear picture of what's going on. Your hemoglobin won't stay up, which is why you're tired. Your blood can't deliver enough oxygen and nutrients to your body. We can do transfusions and drugs. But you can't have a transfusion every time the hemoglobin drops. Your white-blood-cell count is getting close to a dangerous level. We can continue to treat this with drugs.

"Your blood platelets are low, as are all components of your blood. All of these are produced in the bone marrow, and it's been damaged by the cancer and from the side effects of the chemo treatment. The risks with these issues are increasing. Your energy level and your ability to thrive will decrease with the decline in your hemoglobin.

"The lower the white-blood-cell count, the more at risk you are for infection. A simple cold could become life-threatening because your body wouldn't have the resources to fight infection. With a low platelet count, you are prone to bleeding since they are the clotting agents in your blood. If they fall too low, a simple cut or a bruise could have dire consequences because your body won't be able to stop the bleeding. We can give you transfusions of platelets but only so often. And it won't stop the problem.

"So the chemo is now having a worse effect on you than the benefit you're getting from it in fighting the cancer. We need to stop the chemo, and this will allow the bone marrow to recover. And with our help, it can get back up to the levels where the dangers I've been speaking of will be diminished. The obvious downside is that the cancer will progress unabated.

"I don't feel at this time that the end is near, but we have to start discussing how you want to spend the time you have left. If we continue as we have been, you would have to limit or avoid contact with other people to minimize the risk of infections. It wouldn't be advisable to venture out much since a bump—or in the worst case, a fall—could cause internal bleeding.

"I'm not asking you for an answer now. This is something that involves all your family, and I want you to think about it for a few days. Your life tomorrow will be like it has been, and I'll do my best to see that, that continues for as long as possible. But you have to understand and make the plans for when the day comes that you can no longer continue as you have. Sarah, I wish I could say you're cured. Unfortunately, I don't get to do that very often. Do you have any questions?"

Sarah spoke right up. "Well, I once asked you not to gloss over the results. You didn't then, and you haven't now. When you say my life will continue as it has, give me a time period. Just your opinion based on what you know."

"At worst, a few weeks. At best, a couple of months. I can't make any promises."

"I understand," Sarah replied. "What do you mean by making plans?"

"You should get all your affairs in order while you have a clear mind. Finances, a will, that sort of thing. Then I would talk to a hospice care facility and have them discuss with you the services they can provide. They would simply be seeing that you are comfortable and as pain-free as possible. With the caregiver you have"—he looked over at Marla—"you would be able to stay at home. All they want is to know you're not alone."

"Well," Sarah said with a smile on her face, "from what I know of my church friends, I could probably have half an army taking care of me 24-7… I think we should go now, Marla. Thank you, Doctor, for all you've done for me. We have some loved ones we need to tell all this to. Can I call you in a couple of days to discuss this further?"

"That'll be fine. Just continue to take the medications I've been prescribing for you. I'll wait to hear from you," the doctor said. He took Sarah's hand, held if firmly, then released it and left the room.

"No long face today, Marla," Sarah said. "I'm tired. Let's both just compose ourselves and our thoughts. We have to tell Emma and Ed, and that's not going to be easy."

"I know, Sarah," Marla said.

They left and drove home, both deep in thought.

Marla called Ed on the way home. She simply said that they had something they wanted to discuss with him and Emma. Ed didn't ask anything. He knew what was coming. So he simply said that he would be there and that he loved her. Marla told him that she loved him and ended the call.

Emma and Ed were waiting for them when they arrived. Emma was in her place on the couch, and Ed pulled a chair beside them. The girls took their friends' hands as Sarah began to speak. She described the day while Marla sat quietly, amazed at her friend's composure. Emma was unable to hold back the tears, and Marla took a box of tissues off the table and handed it to her.

When Sarah had finished, she reached over and hugged Emma. The embrace lasted for quite a while. Ed took the handkerchief from his pocket and wiped the tears from Marla's cheeks. She continued to look directly at Sarah and her grandmother. And she felt great love for the two women sitting on the couch. Once again, she was reminded that this was not about her.

Sarah and Emma had been close for many years. Long before Marla had arrived on the scene. They were not only close, but they had also grown to feel like kin—like grandmother and granddaughter. Marla felt somewhat selfish. She knew there were many, many other people that would feel as she did when they found out about Sarah's condition now. But Marla knew she and Sarah had a special relationship. She couldn't know how Emma felt, but she cared. She loved Emma and grieved for her now.

While remembering the first time she went to the food pantry with her "old" designer clothes, she recalled watching Sarah interact with all who came in to get the items that were being handed out. She saw Sarah understanding and sharing the feelings of others that day. Marla felt that empathy now. She understood how Emma and Ed felt. The sorrow and sadness in their hearts. And this sorrow would be felt by everyone in their community.

32

EMMA AND SARAH sat together, speaking softly to each other. Marla could only watch, and she knew this conversation was not for her anyway. Instead, she and Ed held hands. They exchanged glances; and when their eyes met, she felt such love. And she sensed that he was feeling the same for her. In spite of the situation, there was joy in her heart. Whatever was to come, Ed would be taking every step that she took, the same as she was doing for Sarah. That knowledge gave her an inner strength. God wouldn't give her what she wanted, but he would provide what she needed. Whatever she had to face, Ed would be right there with her.

Sarah spoke first. "I'll stay home tomorrow morning as I have been. Emma, will you please cancel my week? Marla and I will need to go to my attorney one day and have him make a simple will. I don't have much of an estate. Will you make that appointment, Marla? We need to go over my accounts and bills so that you understand it all and can take over when I'm no longer able. I'll have the attorney draw up a power of attorney and a physician's directive with Marla as the executor of my estate.

"I hope this next Sunday can be one that I can remember. We won't let everyone know the true situation until next week. Is that okay, with you Marla?"

Once again, Sarah give a calm, rational, practical evaluation of the situation. She explained it clearly and confidently, just as she had in the hospital when they were told that she couldn't be cured. *And once again, she looked at me*, Marla thought, *and wanted to know what I thought.*

Marla had learned, and she answered without hesitation.

"Sarah," she said, "I agree completely. We've a lot to do this week. Once it's done, next week, we can all get back to living and enjoying each day that God gives. The rest of the world isn't stopping just because it seems ours may be changing. There's still God's work for you to do. I'm going to do my best to see that you carry on as you have for as long as you are able."

No one said a word. The other three in the room just looked at Marla as if they were thinking, *Who is this woman who just spoke in such a practical way?* This didn't sound like the Marla they knew.

"Marla, I love you. You've really grown in your journey since coming to Waterloo. Remember soon after we met, you told me, 'Oh, Sarah, I've so much to learn,' and you asked me to teach you? I've tried to teach you, and it's obvious that you learned well. I'm so happy for you. Emma and I are so happy for you and Ed.

"And don't look so surprised! We've known for a long time how you all feel for each other. There's nothing the four of us can't face together. Ed, thank you so much for what you've done for me. And standing by Marla through this has made her stronger for me. Now, it's been a long day for me. Marla and I are hungry. Let's all go to the kitchen, grab a casserole of your choice, and dig in."

That brought on a smile to the faces of everyone. Yes, the problem was serious. Yes, there would be hard days coming. But right now, life was good.

*****

On Thursday morning, the girls were getting ready to see the attorney in Greenwood. Marla had called his office earlier in the week, explaining the situation; and they had worked her in. Sarah had gathered all the documents and legal papers she thought she should take. They left and drove to Greenwood. During the drive, there was some simple, pleasant conversation about the weather and a few comments on what they needed to be thinking about to get all of Sarah's affairs in order. Suddenly, Marla changed the subject.

"Sarah, when I first met you, I thought you were something special and wanted to know more about you. As the days and weeks went by, you just never stopped amazing me with your zest for life. I think it became infectious because that's what I began to want for myself. To experience life to its fullest each day.

"That's why it has been hard for me the last few weeks. I couldn't imagine how I could achieve that sense of satisfaction without you beside me. I've learned that it's not where you are in life that's important. It's who you have beside you. With you beside me, I was able to learn the life God wants for me.

"Sarah, I know one day, you'll no longer be with me in person. But you will always be here in my heart. He brought Ed into my life. I don't know God's plans for me and Ed, but it's exciting to think about! I just want you to know that I hope I can face my trials with the same courageous attitude as you. I love and appreciate you, and I'll never forget you."

"Marla, I couldn't have come this far without your help. You've been such a blessing for me. God's truly been at work in our lives. And it worked out the way he wanted because we trusted in him.

"Marla, I want you to know I'm at peace with God. And I believe I've spent my time doing what he wanted me to do. I lived each day with no reserve, no retreat, no regrets."

"I know that," Marla said.

They entered the attorney's office, and Sarah told the receptionist who she was. Mr. Kimbrough was expecting her. He came from his office and greeted them, showing them into a conference room.

The lawyer spoke first. "Sarah, please accept my condolences. I understand what you're going through, not from an emotional standpoint but from a legal standpoint. Unfortunately, I deal with this too often."

"Thank you, Mr. Kimbrough, for your concern. This is Marla, my best and closest friend. I want her to be the executor of my estate and for her to have my power of attorney. I also need a physician's directive," Sarah told of her assets and desires.

Mr. Kimbrough wrote down all that Sarah was saying. He spoke next.

"With your assets and your simple directive, I can draw up a living trust. In South Carolina, you can transfer your assets, such as you have, without having to go through probate. It's pretty straightforward since you own your house and your investment account. At your death, your successor trustee, which you have said you want to be Marla, will be able to transfer the assets to the trust beneficiaries without probate court proceedings.

"I'll draw up all the necessary paperwork and documents and start to work on them immediately. When you leave, give my receptionist your email, phone number, and address. You can send any information I need by email. We can work out all the details this way. When I have everything prepared, I'll send them for you to look over. When you're ready, you and Marla will come back here and sign everything.

"Now, let me see what you brought. I can go ahead and make copies of what I need. Really, just the deed and legal description of the house and statement from your investment account. Marla, I need your driver's license. And, Sarah, your South Carolina ID card."

Mr. Kimbrough took all he needed out to his receptionist to copy.

Sarah spoke up. "Marla, I want you to have the house for many reasons. It's just right that I leave you something, period. We won't discuss the yes or no about this. Maybe when you and Ed get married, you two might want to live there for a while. I don't have much when it comes to worldly possessions. You and Emma take what you would like. Then you do what you think best with the rest of it."

All Marla could do was lean over and hug Sarah. Mr. Kimbrough then returned everything to Sarah. The three of them exchanged pleasantries, and Marla drove them home.

A day's work and Sarah felt a great relief. The more of this she got behind her, the more time she would have for doing more worthwhile things.

33

ON FRIDAY MORNING, the two friends went over to Sarah's house. Sarah went over her bills and files, showing Marla where everything was. Then Sarah called the Hospice of Laurens County and made an appointment for a representative to come visit them.

After lunch, Sarah brought up a great idea. "We have this afternoon free. Let's go to the lake like we used to do! It seems so long ago since we were there." Just like that, their spirts were high, and they both smiled.

"I can't think of anything better or anything else I would rather do. Let's change into our looking-at-the-lake clothes," Marla answered.

The day was perfect for sitting at the lake. Nature's performers did their best to entertain their guests. The adornments of the foliage were exquisitely arranged; they offered beauty for them to experience. It felt like the best day at the lake they had ever had.

*****

Monday, the hospice representative came to the house. "I'm Shirley Albright, a patient advocate with Hospice of Laurens County," the woman said, handing Ed one of her cards.

Ed introduced himself and the other three, gesturing to each one. "This is Sarah. She's the patient. This is Emma, her adoptive grandmother. And this is Marla, her adoptive sister and best friend."

"Pleased to meet you. May I sit down?" Shirley asked.

Sarah said, "Please. Sit by me."

Shirley started the conversation. "Sarah, you gave the receptionist the situation when you made the appointment. One of our nurses contacted Dr. Morgan, and he explained your history and prognosis. We have to verify that you are in need of hospice. We treat patients in their home or at our in-patient facility in Laurens. You've the option of both. We help individuals and families cope so they can get the most of each day and enjoy the best quality of life possible, offering comfort care rather than curative treatment.

"Hospice care focuses on quality of life, and death is viewed as a natural process. We don't hasten nor postpone this natural course. We provide the medication needed for pain and symptom management related to the terminal illness, as well as supplies and medical equipment, such as hospital beds and oxygen, when needed for comfort care."

Shirley continued to explain all the services that would be provided. "We provide the services and are reimbursed by Medicare, Medicaid, and private insurance. But the ability to pay does not limit or hinder the services needed by the patient. We have generous support from the community that covers those expenses the patient can't pay for."

Shirley wanted to know about the living situation and caregivers. She was told that Emma and Marla lived here with Sarah. And if that was not enough, the church had half an army of friends on standby who would be there at a moment's notice.

Sarah and Emma were familiar with hospice care since they had visited or assisted with many members of the church who had gone before them in hospice care. Once everyone was satisfied, Sarah filled out the forms to get the process going. Shirley explained that they would get Sarah's file ready for the day when she thought they should begin to help her. They all visited for a while longer, just giving bits and pieces of each other's side of the situation. After all were satisfied, Shirley excused herself and left.

"Well, I think that's the last detail," Sarah said. "I really feel relieved. Now we can all get busy with life again. I know I'll not be able to do all I would like or all I used to do, but I sure would love if we could all go out to dinner now."

Marla went over and hugged Sarah.

Ed offered, "I would love to take you girls out to lunch. After lunch, if you feel up to it, Sarah, we can enjoy a few hours in Greenville. They have wonderful art galleries, beautiful parks, many things to experience." Their spirits had been lifted. And off they went to Greenville.

*****

On Tuesday morning, Sarah, Emma, and Marla each made a list of five special, close friends to call and explain the diagnosis to. They would all use the same script so as to get the same message across to each person.

The number one statement would be that Sarah's prognosis was *not curable.* But for now, she was the same ol' Sarah everyone knew, and she didn't want to be treated any differently than anyone else in Waterloo. Number two, Sarah wasn't going to have a set schedule but would continue to serve her church, her town, and her community. Number three, they requested that no information other than this be shared with others. Everyone was to remember what the Bible says about gossip.

Sarah was determined to live her life as if nothing had changed. For Sarah, on a day-to-day basis, it hadn't. There was no yesterday. It was gone and couldn't be brought back to life or changed, so why dwell on it? Tomorrow was never promised by God, so why expect it to come? Sarah did what was needed to be done each day and was content with the result because whatever she did, she gave it all she had.

No matter what was discussed with Sarah during this time, all those she spoke with saw Sarah's kindness. She seemed to take a personal interest in what each person had to say, and she wanted to leave that person with a special memory of her.

Life over the next couple of weeks was a joy for Sarah, a joy for those closest to her, and a joy for those whose lives were touched by her. She treasured the evenings and weekends she spent with Marla and Emma. The conversations, as well, were close and personal during this time.

It's hard to describe unless one has been there. There's such joy in just being in each other's presence. Whatever is said, it's always special. Deep down inside, the realities one holds about life must be pressed down. Such realities, if brought forth, would quickly overtake the joy. The mind would then become a battleground, and sadness would take over. *Time is slipping away, and I must do something about it,* one would think. This concern would take control.

Marla knew this. She didn't want to fight this battle although she felt, with her trust in God, she would be able to overcome it. If kept suppressed, out of mind, perhaps the battle would never happen. Marla had learned from Sarah her joy of living for the moment. Sarah had this under control; she let nothing bother her. Marla remembered this. When she had started trusting in God and giving him control, her life had changed. So when fear would creep into her mind, that's when she would go before God and ask him for his peace, which surpasses all understanding.

34

THE TWO GIRLS were spending an afternoon on the back porch. They were enjoying the scene prepared for them by the Creator. All the flora and fauna were on display for them.

"Sarah, do you believe in predestination?"

"What brought this up, Marla?"

"I've been thinking about this," Marla said with a serious look on her face. "I asked you to teach me about God and his love for us and our serving him out of our love for him, for his gift of salvation given to us by his Son Jesus. You've done that. I've found a love in my heart for God that I didn't know before meeting you. You've taught me how to live to serve him. You've taught me how to pray and how to worship. You taught me to simplify my looks, to love others as you do, and now to take over the things you do to serve God. I've been pondering and praying about this the last month.

"I've started reflecting on the changes that have come over me since arriving here. All good and for my betterment. I've continued to watch these changes even until now. Why did all this happen? Was it because it was planned long ago, and it was my destiny to be here?"

Marla stopped talking, and Sarah knew her friend was waiting on an answer from her.

"Marla," Sarah said, "scholars much more learned than I am have been discussing, and debating this subject for thousands of years. I'll give you my thoughts on this. Jesus's work on the cross forgave you of sin, and you can come into the presence of God. His resurrection gave you eternal life through your belief in him by faith. Your righteousness is proclaimed by the life you live and the deeds you do for him. But to answer your question, I believe in free will *and* predestination.

"I think the beliefs are compatible. While one's understanding may be true, it may not be the whole truth. A person delights in thinking he has studied a subject, and he understands it all, and there can be no other truth. Or he fails to believe other truths may exist. One can't understand the mind of God. To study a subject in the Bible and then come up with a personal conclusion of what God meant, when he said it is prideful… I'm no closer to knowing the mind of God than you or any other human.

"Jesus said, 'I am the way and the truth and the life.' The Apostle Paul spoke in the book of Romans that God works for the good of those who love him, who are called to his purpose. I think this has to do with service, not salvation. I believe God predestined the salvation of all humans. And I definitely believe in free will. Satan was with God when he chose to rebel against God, and Satan was created by God. So God gave Satan free will. Satan used it and didn't choose wisely.

"Jesus had free will. God allowed him to be tempted by Satan, and Jesus chose to follow God and disavow Satan. Jesus was not pre-destined to do so. And remember, God said at the creation, 'Let us make man in our image, according to our likeness.' So free will was part of God and his created beings.

"I believe God has wanted all his creation to be with him from the conception of creation. He wanted his creation to *want* to be with him. He could have simply willed it so. God could have created us puppets. He could have created us to perform as he wanted. But he created man with free will. They have a choice. God gave all his creation free will. We can choose life, or we can choose to be separated from life. God wants us all, but not all want God.

"God never eliminated our responsibility in his creation. We, as responsible and intelligent beings, have to choose as God planned for us, not predestined for us on this point. He put us in his plan, and we make choices every day in this journey that he put us on. It always comes down to a choice of two things. We choose good, or we choose evil. We choose God, or we choose the world. You will not get a second chance.

"Marla, you've made many choices since coming to Waterloo. In my opinion, all good. Whether you were predestined to be here or chose to be here, the reality is the same. You are here. We all need to read our Bible, to spend time in prayer and reflection with God, and spend time in worship. But outside of that, one has to make a choice.

"Do I spend time thinking about that which the human mind can never completely understand, or do I spend that time serving God and ministering to his people in need? It's time you went out into this world as Marla, a child of God. I never taught you. I merely helped you to see to make the right choices. God put the will to choose in you, and you chose."

Marla could not speak. Sarah was in a state of special service to God. She was continuing to serve God; and at this moment, it was just directed at Marla, who knew now that she was in the presence of someone really special. She'd known that from the first time she met Sarah. But now, that reality had been taken to a new level.

35

MARLA WAS WITH her teacher, and every day was a joy and a blessing. She thought one day that even Jesus's ministry lasted only three years, a short time that made such an impact. Marla had seen the profound impact her friend was having on the world she was a part of. But each day's work was becoming shorter than the previous. She could see the weariness in Sarah.

Ed often visited them in the evenings. They would sit with Emma and talk about the day. Sarah couldn't last long. Emma usually prepared a plate, took Sarah to her room, and sat with her while she ate. Then she would help with the bath and get Sarah ready for bed. Emma would stay until she saw Sarah's eyes grow heavy with sleep.

Marla and Ed spent such times alone, talking about work. And when Sarah slept late, Marla would run to the office to help with the work. She often told her grandmother just how she felt Sarah was doing.

On Saturdays, the four of them spent time together, if Sarah felt up to it. They sometimes drove out to the lake or strolled in the park, enjoying nature. But Sundays were always about church and worship. Nothing would deter Sarah from this time.

It was Wednesday morning, not much different from some other mornings, when Sarah had told Marla that she was not feeling very well and wanted her pain medicine. After taking it, she told Marla to go to work and come back later. When she returned, Sarah was still in bed.

"How are you feeling?" Marla asked.

"Not too good. That pain medicine helped, but it's like it has worn off already. I don't think I'll be able to go this morning. Will you call and make our apology?" Sarah said with a look that spoke of her discomfort.

"Of course. And then I'll call Dr. Morgan."

"Marla," Dr. Morgan said when he picked up, "I can't prescribe anything more potent than what I have her on now. The body builds up a tolerance to narcotic pain medication, and we have to continually increase the dosage."

There was a long silence.

Dr. Morgan said, "It's time to call hospice. They'll come and visit with you and discuss all that they can do for Sarah."

She backed up to the sofa and sat down. "Goodbye, Doctor."

Emma came in from her room and joined her. She took one look at Marla's face and knew that something was wrong. Marla told her about the conversation she had just had with Sarah and the doctor. They hugged each other and tried their best not to fall apart. They knew they had to go tell Sarah and didn't want her seeing them like this when they entered her room.

After a few moments to compose themselves, they went into Sarah's room. When Sarah saw her friend's face, she knew Marla wanted to tell her something. Sarah had read that face so many times, so she had every nuance memorized.

She patted the mattress beside her. "Come. Sit beside me, Marla, and tell me what you need to tell me."

Marla knew she could hide nothing from Sarah. She sat down on the edge of the bed, looking at Sarah, who only chuckled and grinned.

"I called Dr. Morgan and told him about your pain," Marla said, trying with all her will to control her emotions for just a few minutes. "He said he can't do any more for pain than what he is doing now, and it's time we called hospice."

"Yep, that's what I figured he would say," Sarah said matter-of-factly. "I could tell the last few days that the medicine wasn't working like it had been. I've really had to push myself to make it through the day. I just don't have the strength anymore. The mind is willing, but the body isn't able. Call hospice, and tell them to come. We knew this day was coming. Let's try not to wish it away. Let's do what we need to today. I sure would like to see Pastor Baker today."

This type of scene had been played many times. Sarah was just going to live for the moment and do what needed to be done.

Marla kissed her friend. "Okay." Marla then went into the other room to call hospice and Pastor Baker.

Later, at the office, Marla rushed to Ed and threw her arms around him. She hugged him so tightly that it caught him off guard. He knew the worst had happened, and he gave Marla the embrace she needed. She loved her two friends, Ed and Sarah.

"Ed, we have called hospice. They're on their way over. I need to get back home soon. There's nothing I need to do here now. I'll be working at home most of the time now. I can always leave at times to take care of mail and correspondence, but I want to be with Sarah as much as possible. Please email me what I need to do. You're my rock. Will you come over when you can this afternoon? I want to get back to her now, but I just wanted to see you."

Back at home, Sarah was in bed with her best nightgown on. She had actually put a little blush on her cheeks. Marla stopped in her tracks when she walked into Sarah's room. She thought that Sarah had never looked so beautiful in all the time she had known her.

Sarah was a beautiful girl. That heart of hers just had to show a face of glory now. Marla had always been focused on what was inside Sarah so that she realized she had never really looked at Sarah like she was looking at her now. And she felt a joy and compassion for Sarah she had not felt before. Sarah, always the teacher. Marla, always learning something new from the teacher.

Marla sat down beside her friend on the bed. The two of them had become of one mind so that conversation was not required. At these exact moments, only a look was needed. One hand taking the other spoke volumes. A gentle stroke of one's hand across the forehead of the other was a caress.

The hospice nurse and her companion arrived, and the nurse asked everyone to leave Sarah's room while she examined her. The patient advocate sat down with Marla and Emma in the living room.

There were a couple more papers to sign, and she explained briefly what they could expect while Sarah was in their care.

The nurse returned to the living room a little while later. "She seems to be in good spirits," the nurse stated.

"She's always like that. That's her natural state," Marla said immediately. She didn't know why she had to interject that now, but she was glad she had.

"Well, that's good," the nurse said. "That attitude will help her during the coming days… I've called Dr. Sims, our staff doctor, and given him my diagnosis. He'll be over here to examine her this afternoon and start her on the medications. They'll make her as comfortable as possible. He'll explain all that to you when he gets here. He'll come see her once a week.

"We've many nurses on staff, and one of us will see her in between the doctor's visits. If you feel there is an issue that needs to be addressed, call the office, and a nurse will come over as soon as it can be arranged. There'll be aides who will come over about three times each week to bathe her and change her bed and clothes. They're trained in this so as to minimize the stress on the patients."

They talked a while longer; and when both parties were satisfied, the representatives left.

Pastor Baker arrived soon after lunch and went in to see Sarah. He stayed with her for over an hour. She and Emma sat quietly in the living room, talking about the coming days.

Dr. Sims arrived late that afternoon and examined Sarah. After an extensive exam and some time for conversation with Sarah, he returned to the living room, where Marla, Emma, and Ed were waiting. Dr. Sims sat down with the others with a smile on his face.

"Well, that was a first! It was hard to get into the conversation. She acts like she doesn't need any medication."

Marla said, smiling, "She has joy. It doesn't come in a bottle. Stick around with her awhile, and she'll share a portion of what she has."

The doctor smiled a warm and sincere smile. "I'm sure that's why I came up with the conclusions I did after examining her and talking to her. I usually start the patient off with a mild antidepressant drug. Sarah won't need that. The effects of the cancer and the reality of the situation cause agitation of the body and fog the mind, and I have to treat these symptoms as well. Once again, not with Sarah."

He went on to explain, "She also stated she has no nausea. Her only complaint is pain. She said on a scale of 1 to 10, it's a 3. I can tell the effects pain has on a body and mind. With her attitude and approach to life, I would say it was probably worse than she made it out to be. Anyone else with her pain would have said it was a 6 or 7. I gave her a pill to give some immediate relief to her pain and a patch on her arm with a slow release of a more potent pain medication. The patch usually lasts a week. If it relieves her pain, we'll continue this until something stronger is needed.

"Please don't let her suffer just because she doesn't want to admit it's bothering her. Her pain will get worse as her condition worsens. I can relieve this and see that she's comfortable. She has a big plus going for her with that attitude. The fewer drugs we have to give, the fewer side effects she'll experience—and all the drugs we have to use for this treatment have side effects. We'll treat whatever problems she has. Do you have any questions?"

They were satisfied, and the doctor left. Afterward, they all went in to see Sarah. As always, Sarah spoke up first.

"I wondered where everyone was. I thought you had forgotten I was in here!" Sarah said. "I couldn't ring for you because I knocked the bell off, and it fell behind the nightstand. I knew you'd find me when you came to change the sheets!

"That doctor's a nice man. He really checked me over, and he gave me a pill to help with my pain. He even put this patch on my arm and said it would help with my pain for the rest of the week. His wife's name is Honoria. I just *love* that name. They just returned from a trip to Italy. I always wanted to go there. I didn't get to know much more about him. He didn't talk much."

Sarah stopped talking and looked at Marla and Emma and Ed standing in the doorway. Each of them had that same knowing smile.

Marla spoke up. "Okay, she's fine. Let's go back to the other room. I want to talk about dinner." Then she turned to leave.

"Get back in here!" Sarah shouted at the top of her lungs.

They all broke out in a laughter that brought a sense of peace over all of them, and it lasted well into the evening.

36

MARLA DECIDED THAT in order to conserve Sarah's strength in the days to come, they would start a new routine. This would allow Sarah to concentrate her energy where it was needed the most: her jaw muscles and her lungs. One of their friends had some folding chairs, and they set up four of them in Sarah's room. This way, visitors could come and see Sarah, and it would eliminate Sarah's need to get in and out of bed. The setting was not important but only the conversation. Another friend had a lovely bed table so Sarah could have her meals in bed.

In the afternoons, Marla would take Sarah wherever she wanted to go. They could sit on the back porch, go to the lake, or stroll in the park...whatever Sarah wanted. And so it was for the next couple of weeks. Emma, ever the social scheduler, had the task well in hand. Everyone who wanted to see Sarah (and that was literally *everyone*) was given the opportunity by Emma.

No hierarchy was involved. Everyone knew how special Sarah was. When the visitors were with Sarah, they knew it was a special moment. The love that they saw in Sarah was special, and they knew they would always remember her. Her words were pearls of wisdom to the ears of the listeners.

Every heart that beat in the presence of Sarah was blessed and beat stronger for the experience. She shared something intangible with those who visited. She shared light. But it was not light as we know it by our sun or our technology. She had a light of a far greater magnitude that can't be understood by studying our daily light. She had what Jesus gives. Jesus said, "I am the light of the world. Whoever follows me will never walk in darkness." This light has an effect on those who possess it.

Sarah had it, the light of life. She was a light for all who visited her. Her visitors experienced another quality of this light and its source. The darkness has not understood it and cannot extinguish it. The darkness fears the power of the light and Sarah. And it shunned her. That was the power of Sarah's light: the power over darkness. The darkness did not exist in her world, and so it didn't exist in anyone's world when they were in the presence of Sarah. That's why all who had ever been with Sarah felt a sense of peace and joy when they parted ways with her. The dark parts of their world had left them for a time.

Marla had come to know what each of Sarah's visitors sought and found when they came over to visit. And Marla knew she was especially blessed. She knew this more and more now. Marla, still the disciple, was helping and following her teacher. She was with Sarah when she woke up; and the rays of a new dawn would shine through the back window onto Sarah's bed, as if the sun had been placed in the heavens for just such a purpose. They often enjoyed their breakfast together in this setting.

When the blinds had been opened, the beauty of the outdoors became a show during their meal. Bright-red cardinals and Carolina chickadees would flutter around the birdfeeder that Marla had hung on a shepherd's hook in the yard. The calla lilies showed their colors in the back portion of the yard. After breakfast, the girls would talk about their friendship. God fashions a uniqueness in each of his creations, as well as in every relationship between two people. Each relationship is unique.

The weeks went one by one. Time was moving on, and Sarah's condition worsened a little each day. Her friends understood and accepted it. The daily visits continued, but the durations and the number of visitors were being reduced by Emma. She knew what the girl could tolerate, and she didn't want to push her.

It was difficult for Sarah to get out of bed now. The patio was the limit of her journeys. Marla knew after each effort that it could have been the last. She didn't want that time to come, and neither did Sarah.

In spite of the struggle and pain, she found so much joy in the moments she could be on the back porch with Marla that it was worth the effort. But it was getting to the point where all the willpower that Sarah possessed wouldn't be enough to make that happen again.

As the time with outside visitors passed, the time Marla was with Sarah increased. She was with Sarah for much of her friend's waking hours. Sarah wanted it that way. When Marla had to tend to other matters in life, Emma would take her place. Two people Sarah loved so much were the constant companions in her days now.

The pain could only be diminished, not eliminated entirely. But the medication allowed her to enjoy the companionship of those around her as her world grew smaller.

Pastor Baker came weekly. Then Marla realized that it was just Emma, Ed, and the people from hospice who attended to her needs now. Sarah's strength was diminishing, and her ability to carry on a conversation was gone. But her ability to listen and understand, and the longing to hear Marla speaking, were still strong.

The roles had been reversed. Marla would sit and talk to Sarah. It was always about the two of them, their journey together. Marla would recall the many times she and Sarah had been together and the laughter and joy they always felt during those times. Retelling those moments brought a great sense of peace to Sarah. Other times, Marla would sit and read the Bible to her.

Sarah never took her eyes off her friend. She was content when Marla was there with her. She was fascinated and overjoyed to see the woman Marla had become when she thought back to that first day that the two of them met. Some days, Marla would sit close to the side of Sarah's bed and hold her hand. They would gaze into the eyes of the other or exchange a faint whisper.

Dr. Sims had come over for his weekly visit. After a brief exam, he went back into the living room, where Marla, Emma, and Ed were waiting. "The time is near," the doctor said. "Her body is shutting down. Her kidney and liver function are almost nil. Her breathing is labored. Her strength is almost gone. I'll have a nurse with you twenty-four hours a day. She'll see that Sarah is as comfortable as possible and free of pain. You need to stay by her side now."

The doctor had lived this scene too many times to remember, and he understood the shock of knowing that the inevitable was at the doorstep. He picked up his phone, called the office, and talked to a nurse.

"The nursing staff will rotate someone over here every eight hours. I've heard many wonderful stories from our staff of the times they were here tending to Sarah. Everyone spoke of what a blessing it was to them to have had the chance to be with Sarah."

After that, the doctor let himself out. Marla's numbness had worn off, and she knew she and Emma needed to go in to be by Sarah's side. Her breathing was a struggle, requiring an effort for each breath. The hospice nurse arrived and listened to Sarah's heart and lungs and took her pulse.

"The heart is strong, but she's struggling to breathe," she said.

"She hasn't been alert. Mostly asleep," Marla stated.

"Okay," the nurse said. "I'll be in the other room if you need me."

The three of them sat quietly for a long time. Marla and Emma didn't want to leave for even a minute for fear that Sarah would be gone. Ed went to the living room to answer phone calls. Soon after, Marla called the hospice nurse into the room. Sarah's breathing was now very labored.

The nurse listened to her heart and examined her. "Her time is near. You stay with her."

Marla could hardly grasp the reality of the situation. All the months, weeks, days… They were now down to minutes. "Oh, God, please take this cup from me." Then she realized her mistake. "I shouldn't be asking this of you. But, Lord, your will be done."

She leaned over and, taking Sarah's hand in hers, said with her heart in her throat, "Sarah, please. Please, Sarah, say something." She leaned over and kissed Sarah on her cheek and put her head on Sarah's chest. She could hear the heartbeat. Sarah opened her eyes, and they looked deeply into Marla's eyes.

Her lips started to move as she struggled. "Marla," she said so faintly that Marla could barely hear her. "Marla," she strained to say again.

"I'm here, Sarah. I'm here," Marla said.

"Marla, I want to…tell…you…some…thing." Sarah raised her arm feebly. She seemed to be trying to put her finger on Marla. Sarah strained and put her finger on the center of her friend's chest, where Marla held it.

"I'm here, Sarah. Please tell me."

"Marla…when…to…mor…row…row…starts with…out… without…me…don't think…we…are…are…"—she coughs— "far…a…part…ever—every…time…you…think…of…of… me…I…I…am…right…there…in…your heart."

Her hand fell, and Marla put it back on her friend's chest. Marla was crying. Sarah gathered all the strength she had and said," I… told…you… No tears…"

Marla said, "I'm not crying. Sometimes memories sneak out of my eyes and run down my cheeks."

With the only strength Sarah had left, she smiled at Marla with the smile that Marla knew so well. Their eyes met, and then Sarah's eyes closed. Her diaphragm relaxed for the last time, and Sarah exhaled her last breath. The next she would take would be in a far better place. As the last breath of air left her lungs, a quiet came over the room. A stillness replaced the noise that had been life moments ago.

Emma's, Ed's, and Marla's minds were trying to process what had just happened. Other human minds had faced this same situation for past millennia. Grief tears at the fabric of the heart. The "WHY?" shouted and echoed by all humanity is shouted again. "OH, GOD, WHY? WHY?" No answer ever comes.

The nurse had heard conversation and let herself in. She listened for Sarah's heart, but it beat no more. She noted the time. "I'm sorry for your loss," she said. "Sarah was the most remarkable patient I've ever had. I'll go into the other room. Ed, will you please come in with me soon?" After a while, Ed went in to see the nurse.

The nurse spoke quietly to Ed, "Since the doctor has just seen her, I can pronounce her deceased and fill out the necessary paperwork. I was told you had already made the funeral arrangement, so you need to call the funeral home and have them pick up Sarah's body. I know this sounds unemotional, but it isn't. I find that this is the hardest time in working for hospice. For me, there's always a profound loss. Just not to the degree of the family… I'll send them the death certificate. You need to go tell Marla and Emma what we have discussed." She gave Ed a gentle hug and said, "Take care," before she left.

Ed called the funeral home but asked if they would not rush over. "Maybe wait an hour," he requested. He knew Marla and Emma would need some time with their friend.

"Of course, Ed, of course."

He went back into the room to be with Marla and Emma, waiting a little while before he told them about the funeral home. It was a sad time. It was like all the happiness in the world had left. Marla was in a state of disbelief.

37

I T WAS THE morning of the fourth day since Sarah had gone home to be with her Lord. Marla was getting dressed for the memorial service at 1:00 p.m. Putting the memorial service together had been the thing that had kept Marla going since that moment when her world had stopped. Ed had been her constant companion, taking her everywhere she needed to go to make the arrangements. Meanwhile, Emma stayed home, occupying herself with the phone calls and the many casseroles and soups that were being delivered. Many longtime friends of Emma's were her companions throughout the day, which was what Emma needed now.

Pastor Baker would give the service, and Marla had asked four women to give a testimony about Sarah. Marla told them to speak from their heart, but she also gave each of them something that she wanted said about Sarah. The four women considered that this was one of the greatest honors they had ever been given. Marla knew she wouldn't be able to stand up in front of everyone and say what she felt in her heart without utterly falling to pieces.

Special music had been selected. The Morris sisters would sing two hymns. Sarah had always loved to listen to them whenever they sang in church.

Marla, Emma, and Ed had written Sarah's obituary. This caused Marla great anguish. *How can anyone sum up Sarah's life in two hundred words?* She would type and delete, type and delete. Ed finally told her to give him the points she wanted to make, and he would write it. He did a fine job. Whatever either of them wrote, she knew it would not be adequate, at least in her mind.

Upon talking to the four ladies who would speak about the life that was Sarah's here in Waterloo, Marla was facing the same problem. *How do you retell the memorable moments in the life of someone like Sarah in twenty minutes?* Marla finally knew she had to let it go and trust the four women, having faith that they would do justice to the life of loving and giving that was Sarah's.

Pastor Baker knew Sarah as well as Marla, and she had no doubt that he would speak to the heart of Sarah's life, the love of and service to her Lord Jesus.

When it was time to go to the church, Ed was waiting in the living room for Marla and Emma to get ready. They came in at the same time. Ed could not help but think how beautiful Marla looked at this moment. He gave her a kiss on her lips and Emma a kiss on her cheek and a loving hug.

"Marla, you've made all the arrangements. Everything is planned. There's nothing more you can do. Now, let's go celebrate the life of Sarah with her loving family."

Marla looked at Ed with love in her heart. "You're right, Ed. That's what Sarah would say to me if she could." Marla smiled for the first time since Sarah had passed. They went to the church.

Sarah's casket was in the front of the sanctuary. She had given explicit instructions about her memorial service on two points. She wanted an open casket and she didn't want anyone to send her flowers. "That's the most impractical thing someone could do at such a time," she had said. She had made a list of charities that she wanted donations made to in lieu of flowers.

Marla said that she would abide by her friend's wishes. But she remembered a lesson Sarah had taught about recognizing an opportunity in a situation and taking advantage of it. Since Sarah had said she didn't want anyone to send her flowers, Marla saw the loophole in that statement: Sarah had not mentioned Marla by name, and Marla was not just "anyone." So Marla was not bound to what Sarah wanted from others.

Marla had ordered a beautiful half-casket cover of red roses and a "celebration of life" standing flower spray that the florist had done with every flower she had in her shop. It was stunning. Marla grinned from ear to ear when she saw them. She thought, *Gotcha, Sarah. You taught me well.*

Ed said, "I think she's looking down and smiling at you now. She knows you did it out of love and for no other reason. That's why I wanted to pay half."

"Thank you, Ed," Marla said. They went to the casket and viewed the one they knew and loved so well. Marla only wished this moment would not end.

She broke the silence. "Let's go to the back. It's only 11:45, and I want to talk to Pastor Baker."

They went to the office and found Pastor Baker at his desk. He told them all to come in. They discussed the arrangements, and Pastor Baker assured Marla that everything was prepared as she had wanted. "God's got this," he had to remind Marla. They all prayed; and then the three of them went to the family room in the church, where they would wait until time for the service. Many people stopped by to give their condolences.

The time came for the service to begin; and Julia Baker, the pastor's wife, took them into the sanctuary. All three of them couldn't help but notice that they had never seen the sanctuary filled with so many people. In the pews, people were sitting elbow to elbow. The outside aisles were lined with men standing shoulder to shoulder. They had all given up their seats—most were beside their wives—so that all the women could sit down. It was a humbling sight.

The service went as planned. The testimonies were heartfelt and inspirational. Each was flavored with the humor and the lighter side of Sarah that they all knew so well. One minute, tears were being wiped from eyes; and the next, everyone as laughing out loud at the recalling of some antic of Sarah's. One minute, Sarah could be the epitome of compassion and the next, perform a routine that most standup comics would envy.

The music was perfect. Marla was thinking how she wished she could slow time down to a crawl. She wanted this event to go on and on. She knew that once it was over, it was truly over. The last days had been a blessing, preparing to honor and celebrate the life of a saint.

Pastor Baker began his tribute to the life of Sarah, and Marla could tell he was inspired. He was speaking as if he were talking about the Apostle Paul or Peter. He knew the life of service that Sarah had lived, and he put it out for all to see and understand. Not just in human terms but also in the spiritual sense, which was really what Sarah's life of service was all about.

It was during this part of his eulogy that he paused to regather his composure.

"I have had many remarkable conversations with Sarah through the years I've known her. But the last one we had, I'll never forget. She told me she wanted to read a passage from the Bible but would read it in the first person. She said it was 2 Corinthians 4:16–18. And she read it this way. 'Though my outer self is wasting away, my inner self is being renewed day by day. For this light momentary affliction is preparing for me an eternal weight of glory beyond all comparison, as I look not to things that are seen but to the things that are unseen. For the things that are seen are transient, but the things that are unseen are eternal.'"

Marla was hanging on to every word. This is what she wanted to hear. The reality was that each person already had this knowledge. What everyone thought of Sarah was validated by this man of God, by the Word of God, by the love of God. Sarah could never have attained on this earth the standing that she deserved. But she found it four days ago when she met her Maker, when he opened the Book of Life and found her name written there. He knew her. He looked at her with a pleased look on his face as he said to her, "Welcome, good and faithful servant. I've prepared a room for you."

Marla suddenly felt a joy and a peace that had eluded her the last three days. She realized the truth: Sarah's eternal life had just begun. Why should Marla feel sad while Sarah was feeling the eternal joy of heaven? Once again, Marla had to remind herself, *It isn't always about you, Marla.* She took Ed's hand, squeezed it, and smiled at him. Ed smiled back, happy to see that smile again.

The service ended; and everyone came forward to greet the family, expressing their feelings. Marla witnessed an endless stream of people passing before her. She knew them all, and she felt love for most of them. The rest were good acquaintances. It was as if she were at a huge family reunion, and she was blessed beyond measure.

Everyone then prepared to go to the cemetery. The funeral director had things well in hand. Ed escorted the women to the car, and everyone proceeded to the site. The sheriff's deputies were prepared to stop traffic along the way, but it wasn't necessary. Much of the traffic in town at the moment was in the funeral procession.

38

IT WASN'T A large cemetery, so it took a while for those who came to be able to park. Most had to park along both sides of the highway and walk a bit to the gravesite. Marla, Emma, Ed, and a few close friends who'd been told ahead of time that they could sit in the chairs by the casket were already seated. The pastor was waiting for the rest of the people to make their way to the site. Once everyone had settled around the tented area, Pastor Baker began what was strictly a spiritual message about a life of faith and service, the qualities that spoke to the life of Sarah.

He quoted two scriptures:

> The Lord does not look at the things people look at. People look at the outward appearance, but the Lord looks at the heart. (1 Sam. 16:7)

> "Whoever serves me must follow me; and where I am, my servant will also be. My Father will honor the one who serves me." (John 12:26)

"This was the life of Sarah," he said. He went on to extol the virtues of serving God. "We can't all be like Sarah, but we can all follow in her footsteps." He talked for ten minutes, explaining how we could all be taught by Sarah—not necessarily by her words but by the example she set. After his message, he said a prayer, and the service was concluded. Once again, some of those in attendance passed in front of those closest to Sarah and conveyed their condolences.

Slowly, the crowd dispersed, and people got in their cars to leave. Soon, only Marla, Ed, Emma, and a few people from the funeral home were left. Marla stayed in her chair, thinking of her dear friend. The lessons, the laughter, the tears, the joy, the sorrow, the jokes, the days by the lake and in the park, the aisles of Walmart…all drifted through her memory.

"Marla, we need to leave," Ed stated softly. "Emma is tired and needs to go home."

"I know, Ed," Marla said. "Take Emma home, and then come back. I want to stay here a little longer."

"Okay," Ed answered. "I'll be right back."

Marla sat on the nearby bench and watched the finality of the service of her friend. When Ed approached her again, Marla rose to meet him. She put her arms around him as he embraced her. The tears of sadness began to roll down her cheeks.

"Let it out, Marla," Ed said softly. "I'm here with you."

After some time, relief came to Marla, and she felt like a world of grief had just been cried out. She looked up at Ed and hugged him tightly. *Thank you, God, for this man you brought into my life*, Marla thought. *Thank you.*

Ed looked into her eyes. Looking through the tears, he saw the person he knew he was deeply in love with. "Let's go home," he said.

"I'm ready now. I need to be with Emma," Marla answered.

As they drove home, Marla said, "Ed, I have to take care of Emma now. She can't be alone for a while because she's lost someone special, and I have to take that place."

"I know that," he responded. "Both of us will see to her well-being. I love her too, Marla."

Ed drove them home. They talked as they drove. When they arrived at Emma's house, they found her sitting on the couch.

Marla went to her and hugged her. "Grandmother, I love you, and I'll never leave you. We'll always be here for you. Always. Sarah's gone, but I'm here." Marla looked into her grandmother's eyes and saw what she wanted to see. Emma knew Marla loved her and wouldn't leave her.

The lessons learned from their life with Sarah would always flavor the life that was to come for the two of them. She looked up at Ed and said, "Let's go for a walk." He understood, took her hand, leaned over, and kissed her gently on the lips. They walked forward toward the screen door, opened it, stepped onto the front porch, and into the rest of their lives together. Forever.

The End

About the Author

RAISED BY CHRISTIAN parents in Beaumont, Texas, the author recalls his boyhood fondly. He remembers relatives who lived close by, neighborhood friends with whom he built elaborate tree houses. He also remembers spending time many summers with his grandparents at their fishing cabin on the beach.

Those memories of his youth left an indelible mark on his heart. But it was his faith in Jesus Christ that would give him the strength to deal with the tragedies which lay ahead. Then he would experience the maturing of his Christian faith.

The death of his first wife of forty-eight from cancer left him struggling to cope while working at a building-supply company in College Station, Texas. His three children had all recently married and were starting families of their own.

Though married for a total of fifty years, he was to experience the loss of three beloved wives during that time—two to cancer and the last to stroke. Questions of faith were not easily or quickly answered. But when he served as a hospice volunteer, he was able to find peace that led him to answers of some of those long-held questions. Along with this, the company and counsel of his pastors and friends, time spent in prayer, and Bible study have sustained him.

Tommy Raykovich lives at Hilltop Lakes, Texas. He's a member of Hilltop Lakes Chapel and serves on the board of trustees at the church, enjoying volunteer work in many church functions.

He also serves on the Board of Directors of Hospice Brazos Valley.

CPSIA information can be obtained
at www.ICGtesting.com
Printed in the USA
LVHW091518220322
714101LV00004B/66

9 781639 617616